THE HIDDEN GARDENS OF KYOTO

THE HIDDEN GARDENS
OF KYOTO

Photographs by KATSUHIKO MIZUNO

Text by MASAAKI ONO

Translated by LYNNE E. RIGGS and CHIKAKO IMOTO

KODANSHA INTERNATIONAL
Tokyo • New York • London

EDITOR'S NOTE

The majority of gardens shown here are not open to the public. However, permission to visit imperial or detached palaces may be obtained from the Imperial Household Agency office located near the west gate of Kyoto Imperial Palace. Bring your passport with you, and allow for some delay before receiving permission; this can be as short as one day, but in the high season may take longer. The office is open Monday–Friday, 8:45–12:00 and 1:00–4:00. Most major hotels can help with arrangements, as can Kyoto Tourist Information on the ninth floor of the Kyoto Station building (open 10:00–6:00 every day except the second and fourth Tuesdays of each month; tel. 075-344-3300). Applications may also be made via the internet at sankan.kunaicho.go.jp/index.html

Some temple gardens featured in this book may occasionally be open for limited periods. Inquire at Kyoto Tourist Information.

All Japanese personal names in the text (except those of the photographer, author, and co-translator) are given with the surname first.

The original Japanese edition, *Kyoto hizo no niwa*, was published by Mitsumura Suiko Shoin of Kyoto in 2004.

Distributed in the United States by Kodansha America, Inc., and in the United Kingdom and continental Europe by Kodansha Europe Ltd.

Published by Kodansha International Ltd., 17–14 Otowa 1-chome, Bunkyo-ku, Tokyo 112–8652, and Kodansha America, Inc.

First edition, 2004
10 09 08 07 06 05 04   10 9 8 7 6 5 4 3 2

www.kodansha-intl.com

CONTENTS

Villas, Inns, and Restaurants   93

PREFACE

Katsuhiko Mizuno

Compared to the gardens of Europe and the Islamic world and despite the strong influence of those of China, Japanese landscape gardens have their own distinct forms, of which impressive examples may be found in Kyoto. While evolving through various phases of development, they reflect a tradition that goes back to the beginning of recorded history and continues even today.

Part of the fascination of Japanese gardens is that they can be discussed in terms of one more-or-less consistent stylistic tradition even though they are quite diverse in form. This consistency in diversity can be said to reflect the natural scenery on which they are modeled. Whatever their format, they utilize three basic elements—rocks, water, and plants—to recreate the essence of real landscapes, sometimes realistically, sometimes abstractly, in a subtle balance between the natural and the contrived that eludes conscious analysis.

Since time immemorial, the Japanese have loved, respected, and feared nature, as well as worshiped it as a source of strength and solace. For those who lived by the sea, gardens were places to dig ponds and make islands enshrining the gods of the sea. People in the steep inland areas were responsive to the powerful presence of large rocks and believed them to be the abodes of the gods. Examples of these early forms of nature worship can be found today in the sacred pond and islands on the grounds of Inou shrine in Suzuka, Mie prefecture, and in the rocks venerated at Matsunoo shrine in Kyoto's Sakyo ward.

The garden traditions of China and the Korean peninsula entered Japan along with the influx of continental culture accompanying the introduction of Buddhism during the Asuka period (552–645). Ancient Chin and Han dynasty legends about the sacred mountain of Penglai (Horai in Japanese), where the immortals were said to dwell, inspired the development of the pleasure boat style of garden centering around a lake or pond, in which islands were built to evoke Mt. Horai or the crane and tortoise—symbols of longevity and fortune.

As history moved on, through the Nara period (710–794) and into the Heian period (794–1185), the architecture of the elite developed into the *shinden* style, consisting of a central hall connected by corridors to various pavilions and other structures in a meandering complex set in spacious grounds. In these settings, the pleasure boat style of pond garden reached its height. This was the era when so-called "meandering stream banquets" (*kyokusui no en*) became fashionable among the aristocracy, at which guests were invited to compose verses before a cup of wine set adrift upstream floated down to them.

The same period was one in which a pervasive pessimism set in, triggered by the Buddhist teaching that the world was entering an age of moral decline. The numerous "Pure Land" temple gardens, devised to replicate the Paradise of the Amida Buddha, were a reflection of this mood. The pond garden at the Byodoin Phoenix Hall is one of many examples of this style.

As the warrior class became ascendant in the subsequent Kamakura period (1185–1333), the mainstream of architecture shifted from the *shinden* to the more moderate scale of the *shoin* style of dwelling. In place of vast gardens with ponds designed for boating, the preferred style of pond garden switched to one more intimate in size and intended for strolling. Also, as the Zen sect of Buddhism spread rapidly through the warrior stratum of medieval society, gardens went from scenes of leisurely amusement to places of spiritual contemplation. The Zen garden, perfected by the priest Muso Soseki (1275–1351), was soon found throughout the country.

During the Muromachi age (1333–1568), the shogun Ashikaga Yoshimitsu commissioned a palace in the Kitayama section of Kyoto, known for its Kinkaku or golden pavilion, which after his death became the temple Rokuonji. A later Ashikaga shogun, Yoshimasa, built the palace in the Higashiyama area that became Jishoji temple, famous for its Ginkaku or silver pavilion. For ten years in the middle of this period, however, civil war raged through the city, and many of the fine gardens created there by powerful warlords were destroyed. It was no coincidence, perhaps, that some of the great dry landscape gardens such as those at Ryoanji and Daisen'in temples, noted for the striking tension of their rock arrangements, were designed in the wake of that turbulent time.

The opulent culture of the Momoyama age (1568–1603) that

followed also left its mark on gardens, and examples of bold stone arrangements created in gardens of that time remain, for example, in the Kokei no Niwa garden of Nishi Honganji temple (p. 36). Japanese gardens reached their zenith during the peaceful centuries of the Edo period (1603–1868) in the gracious and expansive gardens of princely estates, the highly refined dry landscape gardens of temples, and the stepping stone gardens of teahouses, with their carefully calculated and imaginatively contrived rusticity.

Even after the nation's capital moved to Tokyo in 1868, a major Kyoto public works project that involved building a canal from Lake Biwa in the north was completed, channeling a steady supply of irrigation water to the eastern suburbs of the city. It was at this time, at the turn of the twentieth century, that landscape artist Ogawa Jihei (1860–1933) introduced fresh ideas into the world of garden design with innovative projects influenced by Western-style gardens. In the next generation, Shigemori Mirei, an advocate of what he called "timeless modernism," created dramatic works based on designs reaffirming the role of stone arrangements. In our own time as well, gardens continue to be built that reflect both the creative imagination of modern designers and the rich traditions that have been passed down to them.

The climate and geography of Kyoto provide everything the Japanese-style garden requires. The stones used, for example, must be natural, and a plentiful supply of the sedimentary rock called chert can be found in the mountains surrounding the city. The pebbles indispensable to the composition of dry landscape gardens, called Shirakawa gravel, are the natural product of the current of the Shirakawa river, which breaks up and rounds off granite boulders as they are washed down from Mt. Hiei. This same granite was carved to create garden lanterns and basins, and became especially popular in the Edo period after it was used by tea master Sen no Rikyu. Taiko-ishi, the stone favored by the powerful warlord Toyotomi Hideyoshi, is a particularly prized type of Shirakawa granite.

The Kyoto basin is one of few places in Japan where rocks of a number of different compositions may be found in close proximity. The rivers to the north of the city, for example, yield what are called the "seven Kamo stones," including the black Yase granite of the Takano river, the Kurama granite of the Kurama river, Kibune schalstein from the Kibune river, and the pink Kamo chert from the river of that name. The skillful placement of one fine ornamental stone from the Kibune river or the creation of a *tsuboniwa* with a water basin, step-up stone, or other stone features is sufficient to evoke within a small space the particular attributes of the Kyoto landscape.

In terms of climate, the hot, humid summers and cold winters of the Kyoto area provide good conditions for the growth of the trees and shrubs favored for local gardens. Flowering trees like the plum and cherry, shrubs like camellias, as well as evergreens like the red pine and cedar flourish, and the haircap moss that shows off to best effect the beauties of dry landscape gardens thrives on the cold mists of Kyoto's winters.

Above all, however, these gardens have survived because of the uninterrupted care over more than a thousand years by generations of owners, landscape designers, and gardeners. They have kept the flow of funds from drying up, sustained the supply of artistic talent, and maintained the high technical standards needed to create and preserve the gardens. It may be no exaggeration to say that this care extends not only to well-known gardens, but to the backyard plots of modest urban homes as well, which reveal the average inhabitant's pride in the city's heritage.

Most of the gardens pictured in this book are not ordinarily open to the public, thus representing another face of Kyoto, off the beaten track of the casual tourist. Access, however, can be obtained by various means. Those wishing to visit imperial villa gardens may apply to the Imperial Household Agency for special permission at the office attached to Kyoto Imperial Palace, or via a hotel or travel agency. Guests who dine or stay at fine inns and restaurants can also enjoy some impressive gardens which, precisely because they are protected and private, have managed to preserve much of their original beauty.

Kyoto Imperial Palace, bush clover garden

In 794, the imperial capital was moved to Heian
(later known as Kyoto), in a setting of pleasant hills
and pristine rivers, where it remained for 1100 years.
There, culture and arts steeped in the beauties
of nature and its cycle of seasons were fostered
and refined over eleven centuries. Born also out of
a deep love of nature, Kyoto gardens in a way
encapsulate the history of Japanese landscape
gardening as a whole. This chapter includes
the gardens of imperial palaces, tea masters,
as well as shrines.

KYOTO IMPERIAL PALACE, SEIRYODEN EAST COURTYARD

Light reflected from the white pebbles of the courtyard intensifies the green of the bamboo foliage. Renewing itself each year, bamboo embodies permanence in change, making it the perfect planting for this building that was the regular home of the emperor. In the combination of the purity and simplicity of pebble-covered space and the stately beauty of bamboo may be found one of the ultimate forms of the Japanese landscape garden.

The priest Yoshida Kenko, in essays written around 1330 reminiscing about life in the capital in his time (*Tsurezuregusa*), attests to the presence even then of a growth of *kuretake* (black bamboo) near one of the buildings and another of *kawatake* (river bamboo) near the surrounding water drainage channel. In ancient times, there was another structure situated opposite the Seiryoden, called the Jijuden, and the fact that the black bamboo (center) was originally attached to the Jijuden while the river bamboo (left) belonged with the Seiryoden might explain why today the two plantings are not more symmetrically placed.

KYOTO IMPERIAL PALACE, OIKENIWA POND GARDEN

In a garden with a pond spacious enough to allow pleasure boating, the approach from the boat landing to the garden is an important scenic feature. Here, accenting the expanse of rocks spread over the sloping beachhead, a path of large, unevenly shaped stones leads down to the water's edge, recreating the ambience of a seashore. One of the key compositional features in the beauty of a pond garden is the handling of the pond's edge. Garden designers turn to various elements—arrangements of natural stones, cut stone, bank-retaining weirs (*shigarami*), and plantings of grasses (*kusadome*)— but surely a stony shore makes for the most impressive perimeter. A considerable amount of land is needed, given the distance needed to absorb the difference in height between the land and the surface of the water, so few gardens other than those on the spacious grounds of a palace can achieve this effectively. Of course, as also exemplified at Sento Imperial Palace and Katsura Detached Palace, it was precisely this sort of scene that best suited the gardens of the imperial family.

SENTO IMPERIAL PALACE, NORTH POND GARDEN
(SIX-SLAB BRIDGE AND AKOSE POOL)

After passing through the elegant scenery of the open spaces, in this part of the garden the visitor has the unexpected pleasure of entering an area of quiet seclusion. Perhaps because it is believed to be the site of a natural spring located here before even the palace was built, this corner has a certain mystique to it.

◀ **SENTO IMPERIAL PALACE, SOUTH POND SHORE**

Featuring a design similar to the stone-paved shoreline of the pond at Kyoto Imperial Palace, this beach is even more generous in scale and gradual in gradient, curving off endlessly into the distance. The lake edge arcs wide and unobstructed, the epitome of courtly grace. Indulging solely in this curve, the design is left uncluttered by rock arrangements that might break its continuity. The proportions between the expanse of water and the area of the shore are well balanced, creating a landscape both elegant and sweeping in scale. Here is Kobori Enshu at his best.

KATSURA DETACHED PALACE, SHOKINTEI FOREGARDEN

Here the scene shifts from a path winding through hills to this landscape of open water. At the tip of the rocky point stands a promontory lantern and beyond it the thatched roof of the Shokintei teahouse toward which the path leads. The teahouse is plainly visible in the distance, but the red pines and the line of islands in the water, evoking the famed Amanohashidate landscape of Wakasa Bay (in northern Kyoto prefecture), distract and obstruct one's gaze, creating the illusion of a pavilion far away and difficult to reach. The two bridges connecting the islands to the land, the Hotarubashi made of cut stone and the Tsukimibashi made of natural

stone (far right), further augment the sense of distance. While one's attention is drawn to the Amanohashidate-like scene across the water, the stepping stones around the pond lead past the Oribe stone lantern sunk deep into the ground to one side (upper left corner). Further along the path, one turns right and proceeds over the long span of the Shirakawabashi bridge, then steps down to wash one's hands in the pond's in-flowing stream before moving on to the crawl-in entrance (*nijiriguchi*) of the teahouse.

KATSURA DETACHED PALACE, SHOIKEN FOREGARDEN

This is a view of the Shoiken teahouse across the pond past the "snow-viewing" lantern at one side of the Ume-no-baba bridle way. The banks of the pond here are not retained with self-assertive stone arrangements, but with serene slabs of cut stone that emphasize horizontal lines, paralleling the elongated proportions of the Shoiken. No other conspicuous arrangements impose; it is simply a quiet mooring place. At Katsura Detached Palace, with all its meticulously planned aesthetic details, the gentle unpretentiousness of this scene is pleasantly restful. The placing here of a "snow-viewing" stone lantern of an unusual shape, without the usual bulb (known as a *hoju*) on top but with only a slight circular bulge at the peak of its roof-stone, may also be intended to enhance the tranquillity created by an emphasis on the horizontal.

SHUGAKUIN DETACHED PALACE, UPPER VILLA
YOKURYUCHI POND AND CHITOSEBASHI BRIDGE

Looking east from the western side of the pond, with Mt. Shugakuin in the background, one sees Chitosebashi bridge, a covered span made of one large rock laid upon pinions of cut stone allowing access to Banshou island. This does not date from the time the estate was built by retired Emperor Gomizuno-o (1596–1680), but appears to have been added in 1824. Visible at the center of the photograph is a resting place on Banshou, its red painted panels standing out in the surrounding greenery. Further to the right is the Rin'untei teahouse, floating above the trimmed shrubbery.

◀ **SHUGAKUIN DETACHED PALACE, UPPER VILLA OVERLOOK AND**
YOKURYUCHI POND

Climbing the stone steps through dense growths on either hand, the path emerges at this splendid vantage point. The foliage that had masked the view up the incline gives way to a massive hedge, trimmed back to expose a panorama of the "pool where dragons bathe" (Yokuryuchi). The vast, deep pond looks perfectly natural, although it is actually an artificial lake created by damming a stream. Gazing across the pond at the hills in the distance from the Rin'untei teahouse, one feels as though one were literally floating on clouds—an effect made possible by the swath of trimmed shrubbery that cuts off sight of ground level.

OMOTE SENKE, ZANGETSUTEI FOREGARDEN

To the left, beyond the bed of pine needles beneath the red pine, is the wall of an old well, a *kuro-moji* (spicebush) fence, a thatch-roofed gate (*kayamon*), and a hexagonal stone lantern. To the right is visible the cedar-bark shingled *nakakuguri* gate between the inner and outer gardens; the space between the two gates is divided with a hedge curving in the shape of the letter C. The Zangetsutei occupies the pivotal position within the Omote Senke garden; the *nakakuguri* gate leads out to the exterior resting place and the entrance to the garden while the *kayamon* leads to the Tensetsudo founder's hall and its garden. Despite the various structures that dot the Zangetsutei grounds, the C-shaped hedge manages to curve gracefully through the space without making it feel crowded. When a number of buildings face the same garden, sharing its space, one of the focal points for the garden connoisseur is the way these space dividers have been arranged. One of the attractions of the Omote Senke garden is the successful way in which it is subdivided yet at the same time integrated as one large garden.

◀ **OMOTE SENKE, FUSHIN'AN TEA GARDEN**

A significant feature in the appreciation of a tea garden is the arrangement of stones for the path leading through it. The path through the Fushin'an garden includes some smaller, extra stones that diverge from the main course. The small one behind and to one side of the step-up stone immediately in front of the crawl-in entrance is one example, and, four stones back, the small stone accompanying the branch off to the sword rack (not shown) to the left is another. It may be that these were added to ease the visitor's passage, as none of the individual stones is large; yet one wonders if they weren't placed there less for practical than aesthetic reasons, as subtle touches to the scenery. The presence of such supplementary stones makes the path more than simply a straight line leading toward a desti-nation, and helps them harmonize with the surrounding moss. The extra stone close to the step-up stone at the entrance is a frequent feature of Omote school tea gardens.

URA SENKE, PATH FROM FRONT GATE TO ENTRANCE

Entering the gate and moving along the path paved with small stones in a pattern known as *arare-koboshi*, a term evoking the effect of spilled pellets or beads, the stones soon curve to the right and trace a straight line to the entrance. In this stretch the visitor confirms the feeling that the secular world outside has been left behind. Between the high hedge along the left side and the thick growth of *kumazasa* (striped bamboo) on the right lies an alley of just the right width and of sufficient extent and atmosphere to compose one's mind in preparation for entering the secluded world beyond. Perhaps constructed as a makeshift means of keeping the shrubbery from drooping onto the path, the simple bamboo fence of poles lashed together at two levels adds a rustic touch to the scene. This is the sort of touch, in fact, that is especially necessary in a tea garden.

URA SENKE, YUIN TEAHOUSE FOREGARDEN

If not told beforehand that it was a Senke teahouse, one might find this thatch-roofed structure more reminiscent of the rustic farmhouses to be seen in the surrounding hills. Inscribed on a placard in its gable are the characters *yuin*, meaning to "retire once more," and the building is in a style well suited to its name. The Yuin teahouse is famous for the stepping stones in its foregarden, set in a seemingly random, "scattered bean" (*mame-maki*) pattern. In a garden of limited size, when the paths lead off in various directions (here, to the crawl-in entrance, the hand-washing basin, the sword rack, and the path along the side of the building) the landscape would become cluttered if individual lines of stones were set leading this way and that. Instead, the entire area is sparsely covered with stones. Despite the larger number used, they fit the space nicely, and though the stones may seem to be where they are by chance, in fact they are exactly where they need to be. Like all the best designs, this involves a subtle balance between the calculated and the casual.

MUSHANOKOJI SENKE TEA GARDEN

The Amigasa-mon gate, with the unusual curve of its cypress-bark roof, has enough presence in itself to characterize the singular world of tea, but the simple open structure of the bamboo-slat gate and the Zuiryu-style wing panel prevents it from being too conspicuous. Through this gate, to the left, one comes to the Kankyuan entrance, while the path past it on the right leads back to the waiting bench. The temple foundation stone under the gate is a threshold stone (*tozuri-ishi*). The host, waiting inside at the stone off to the left of the gate, greets the guest pausing at the large stone outside in the foreground. The name of the teahouse (Kankyu, or Kan o yasumu) suggests that the owner has retired from official service to pursue the way of tea.

MUSHANOKOJI SENKE, SODO FOREGARDEN

The eaves extending from the Sodo (founder's hall) on the right rest on a half-wall (*koshikabe*) with a lattice window. Another wall protrudes from the right corner of the hall, creating an enclosed space (*tsubo-no-uchi*) that is prototypical of the small tea garden. A *sudare* blind conceals the entrance for special guests, its large stone step visible below. On the far side of this four-and-a-half-mat room is a shrine to the tea master Sen no Rikyu.

YABUNOUCHI SOKE, WAITING SEAT

For the special or main guest at a tea gathering, this waiting spot has a seat set aside in a wing around the corner from the body of the building where other guests would be seated. Whereas, in most cases, the guest of honor is seated at the head of a linear arrangement, here the seat is separated from the rest. The Yabunouchi family had close ties with Nishi Honganji temple, and this design may have been in consideration of the fact that the head priest was a frequent visitor. The guest-of-honor stone (*kinin-seki*), moreover, is of particularly generous size and height. The right side of the seat is a windowed wing wall and the left side is curtained off with a woven mat that serves to conceal a person of special rank. The straw hat hanging on the wall at the left is for the use of guests entering the garden on a rainy day.

YABUNOUCHI SOKE EN'NAN, WATER BASIN

Moving along the stepping stones from the waiting area shown on the previous page, one passes the *mitsukosode-ishi*—a stone from Sen no Rikyu's garden that Yabunouchi Kenchu (1535–1627) is said to have traded for three kimono—then comes to a simple wooden *sarudo* gate, before entering the En'nan inner garden. The water basin here is known as the Mongaku stone and is believed to have been made from part of a stupa erected for the repose of the late twelfth-century priest Mongaku's soul. The appointments in this garden reflect the host's devotion to honoring his guests in every way. The stone in front of the basin is in the shape of a finger pointing, and it is there that the host would stand to dip water and pour it over the hands of an honored guest. Behind the basin is an Oribe-style lantern and beyond that a bamboo fence (*taimatsu gaki*).

FUSHIMI-INARI GRAND SHRINE, MATSUNOSHITAYA GARDEN

Matsunoshitaya is the name of the former residence of the Matsumoto family, priests of the Inari Grand Shrine in Fushimi, and the east garden is named after this residence. In the north of the garden is a teahouse that is believed to have been in Sento Imperial Palace, built by retired Emperor Gomizuno-o. A path links this structure with another teahouse, called Zuihoken, on top of an artificial hillock at the foot of the Inariyama hills. With its long, narrow channel dug north and south to pool water draining from the foothills and its use of old temple foundation stones, the garden has the flavor of a villa garden of a kind that was popular at the turn of the last century. It is thought that the Matsunoshitaya garden was completed sometime in the Taisho era (1912–1926).

FUSHIMI-INARI GRAND SHRINE, OFFICE GARDEN

The pond is long and narrow, running the length of a guest hall stretching north and south. A raft-style stone bridge leading from the large temple foundation stone on the near bank over the water, and another stone bridge beyond it, form a path to the other side of the pond. Although a stone lantern is usually intended to draw one's attention in one particular direction, the use of several scattered about a garden, as seen here, is an interesting variation.

Gokonomiyajinja shrine, guest house garden

An Oribe-style stone lantern accompanies the large water basin in this dry landscape (*karesansui*) garden. Beyond the lantern is a fine example of a waterfall rock arrangement. In a typical garden the rocks used are of the same type and color, but this one, laid out in relatively recent times, was designed with a variety of rocks left over from the building of Fushimi Castle. The water basin, too, was made from a large stone in the castle wall. The trees consist principally of *goyomatsu*, a Japanese white pine, though they include the five-color camellia, a variety favored by Kobori Enshu. The garden is the work of a man trained from the beginning of his career with the gardeners retained for upkeep of the shrine's gardens.

Kohoan temple, *takeyarai* fence

The main compositional elements contributing to the beauty of gardens may be rocks, sand, trees, shrubs, and moss, ponds and streams, but many other elements come into play—stone water basins, stone lanterns and bridges, hedges, fences, and so forth. These combine to produce a fine landscape garden. Kyoto is the wellspring of the Japanese garden tradition, and its temples commissioned by far the largest number of them, as shown in the following pages.

Daitokuji main temple, Hojo south garden

In order to secure an uncluttered way between the Chokushi-mon (Envoy's Gate) and the Hojo (usually the senior monks' living quarters), no garden stones or shrubbery could be placed there, so only an expanse of white gravel with a pair of cone-shaped mounds is to be seen. As is typical of the south garden of a Hojo, the rock arrangements and plantings are limited to the fringe of the garden wall. Since the garden could be viewed from opposite sides—from both the Hojo and the Chokushi-mon—priority was given to the prospect from the Hojo. Situating rock arrangements close to the south wall had the advantage of assuring that the view from the Chokushi-mon would not be of their back sides. At the same time, since Hojo halls were often built with high floors and wide verandas, unless the rock arrangements were situated some distance away, they would not be visible from inside.

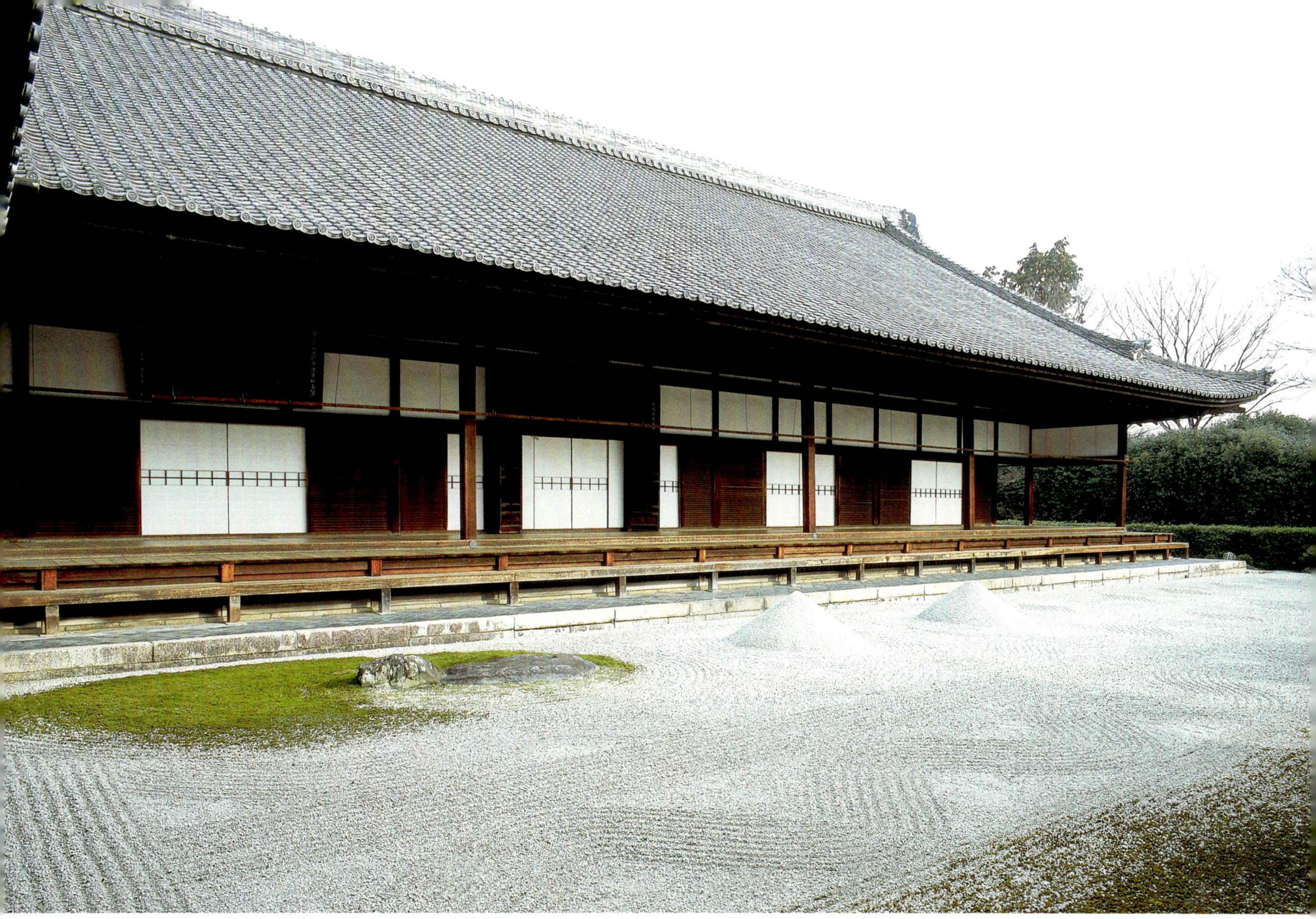

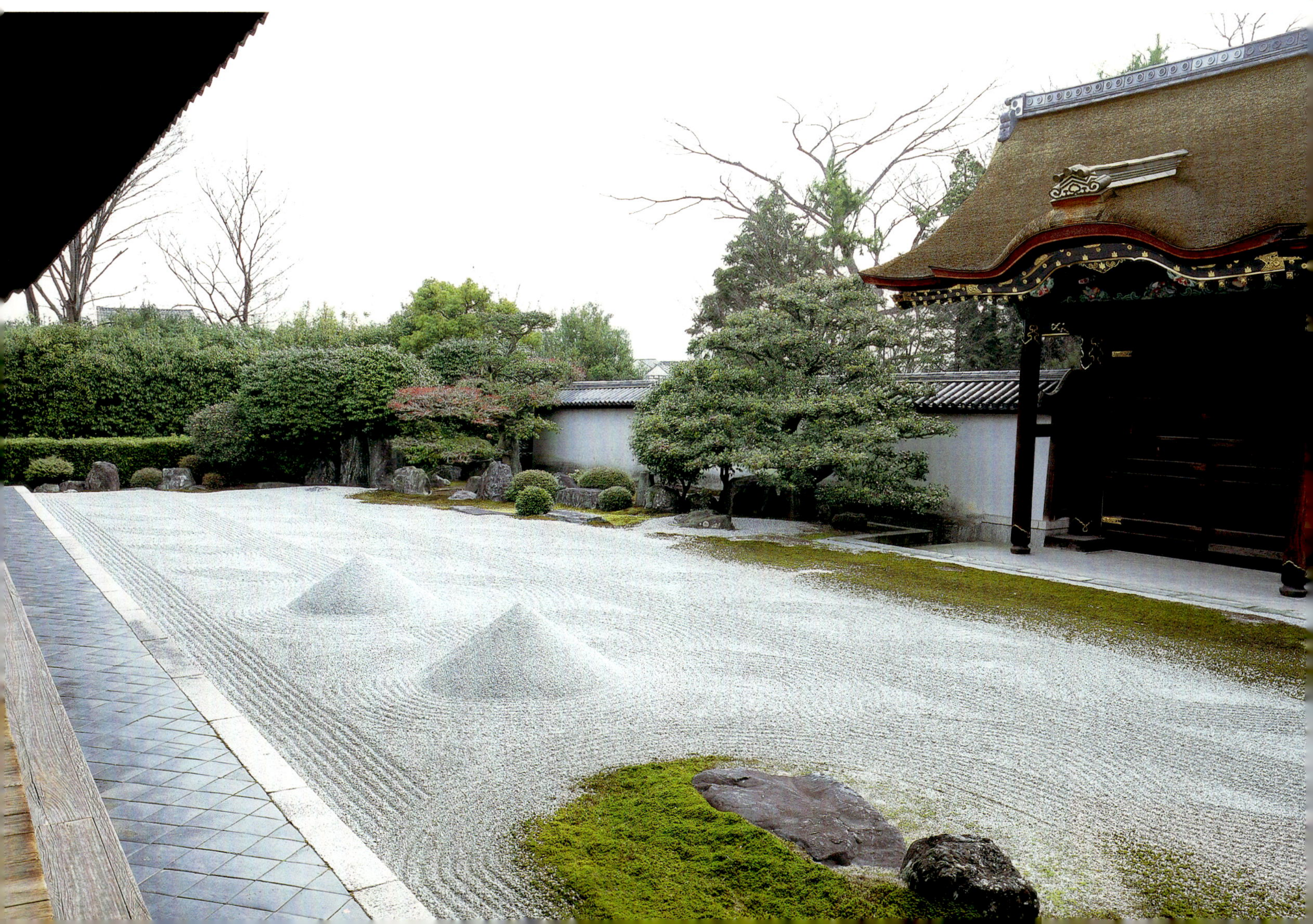

DAITOKUJI MAIN TEMPLE, HOJO EAST GARDEN

When the garden lacks depth vis-à-vis the floor level of the hall and the breadth of the veranda, the scenery might be virtually out of sight from within the building, and only the tops of upright rock arrangements would be visible, with awkward results. The solution devised in this case is a seven-five-three arrangement of rocks such as in a bonseki tray garden, centering around horizontal stones (*yoko-ishi*) and recumbent ones (*fuse-ishi*) that are attractive when viewed from a high vantage point. From inside the building, one can't help gazing off over the hedges toward the outside. The double tier of hedges serves as an effective technique for incorporating the outside area into the landscape of the garden, because the hedges blend well with outside greenery. The double row of hedges makes it easier to adjust the height appropriately, augmenting the volume of greenery so as to attain a balance between the inside and outside. The scenery thus "borrowed" once extended to Mt. Hiei, lying off beyond the trees.

SHINJUAN TEMPLE, TEIGYOKUKEN OUTER TEA GARDEN

Passing along the stepping stones with a podocarp tree on the left and a Ternstroemia japonica on the right brings one to an entrance beyond which lies an inner courtyard furnished with a water basin and sword rack. To illuminate the space enclosed by the walls and the pent roof is a lattice just above the entrance. There is also a skylight in the shingled roof, while just visible in the wall behind the podocarp is an exposed-wattle window (*shitaji mado*). The water basin is on the other side of it. Each feature for introducing light is both useful and harmonizes well with the scene.

JUKOIN TEMPLE, HOJO SOUTH GARDEN

Looking at the group of rocks on the left, one notes two standing stones (*tate-ishi*) to the left and right of the horizontal stone shining white in the sun. The higher right-hand one and the upright stone beyond it are set at a slant, suggesting the wings of a crane. The four stones in this area are similar to the arrangement in the Reiun'in garden at Myoshinji temple. Since rock arrangements rarely diverged from the rules established by earlier masters, it is believed that the two gardens were either designed by the same person or by a follower in the same tradition. The above-mentioned Reiun'in garden is known, from records preserved at that temple, to have been designed by Shiken Seido (1486–1581) of Shokokuji temple. One theory is that Jukoin temple garden was designed by Sen no Rikyu, but there is a good possibility that Shiken made the gardens at both temples, since although he would have been eighty years old in 1566 when Jukoin was built, he lived on for another fifteen years.

JUKOIN TEMPLE, HOJO SOUTH GARDEN

The view is from the southeast side of the Hojo garden, looking toward the Hojo. The two large standing stones in the center form the "wings of the crane" mentioned on the previous page.

KOHOAN TEMPLE, BOSEN-SEKI WEST GARDEN

The theme of Kohoan's garden as a whole is the landscape of Omi (in present-day Shiga prefecture), featuring scenes around Lake Biwa. This corner evokes the lakeside scenery as viewed from passing *yakatabune* pleasure boats. The long, narrow space framed by the veranda, its one-step-down extension, and shoji panels open at the bottom all contribute to a sense of looking out from a wooden boat. The water basin, named Roketsu ("dew-catching"), is well positioned vis-à-vis the stone lantern, which makes the scene loom larger than life. The stone beyond the lantern, in the shape of Mt. Fuji, could simply be a back stone for the water basin, or it may be meant to evoke the mountain landscape on Lake Biwa's north shore famous in poetry and art as "Omi Fuji."

Beyond the shrubbery, the space opens out onto the Jiki'nyuken south garden. One can only admire the way a mere corner of a larger garden has been fashioned into a little masterpiece.

KOHOAN TEMPLE, JIKI'NYUKEN SOUTH GARDEN

In striking contrast to the scene captured within the small space of the Bosen-seki garden, here the landscape opens wide. The line of vision focuses on a stone bridge located in the center, its low height further emphasizing the illusion of distance. The angle at which the bridge is placed, moreover, is calculated to cut a diagonal that will draw attention even from afar. The presence of the bridge signals that the gravel expanse symbolizes water, evoking, as one might expect, Lake Biwa.

KOHOAN TEMPLE, SAN'UNJO TEAROOM GARDEN

Between the Oribe-style stone lantern at the rear and the coin-shaped (*fusengata*) water basin are two overlapping horizontal stones of the lamp-lighting (*hiage*) style, accompanied by small evergreen oak and Japanese pieris shrubs. These elements, set with exceptional skill, bring the scene around the basin into a cohesive whole. A similar treatment may be seen in the *hiage* stone found also before the lantern in the Bosen-seki garden (pp. 28–29); the arrangement with the lantern planted firmly amidst foliage helps to give a sense of stable serenity to the scene. The name of the tearoom evokes a passage from the Buddhist classic *Hekiganroku* (Blue Cliff Record) relating to water.

HOSHUN'IN TEMPLE, HONDO FOREGARDEN

In a vast sea of white gravel floats a ship of stone against a background of what must be the legendary peaks of Horai (Penglai), land of the immortals. In front of the largest rock is a *rigyo-seki* stone suggesting a carp surfacing by a waterfall. The stones with flattened tops arranged at the right suggest the various stages of the cascade. This waterfall arrangement appears to follow the pattern found also in the Daisen'in and Shuon'an gardens. The moss-covered hillock to the right adds a soft, elegant touch. The weight of the rock arrangement is shifted somewhat to the right, with the design opening out and flowing more loosely toward the left, reveling in the empty space.

Hoshun'in temple, Donkokaku garden

The two-storied building in the center, called Donkokaku, has a covered bridge called Dagetsukyo to one side of it. In the middle of the Houn'-ike pond in front is an island from which a pair of stone bridges pivot at an angle. This angled bridge layout, evoking the hiragana character *ku* (〈), is a design technique often used in small gardens. If the bridges stretched straight across the area, the visual effect would be uninteresting and considerable space would be needed to make it attractive. Achieving a genuine balance between the height of a pavilion and its surroundings is also only possible in spacious grounds such as provided for the Kin-kaku and Ginkaku pavilions. On this smaller site, the designer seems deliberately to have used the disproportionately large pavilion to break the compositional equilibrium, making it loom up like a mirage. This is a garden that disorients.

KORIN'IN TEMPLE, HOJO GARDEN

This garden was built by Nakane Kinsaku at the time the Hojo was dismantled and repaired in 1975. Nakane based his design on illustrations of a garden owned by the Hatakeyama clan (patrons of the temple) that appear in an old source called *Tsukiyama teisaku den* (Treatise on Hill Garden Design). The garden presents the scene of two ranges of hills to left and right, with a dry gully in between and a bridge at the back between the hills. This style of garden was fashionable in the Momoyama period (1568–1603), as also seen in the nearby Kanjiin temple garden (p. 39) and the Ninomaru garden at Nagoya Castle. The two stones planted in the white gravel are, at right, a wave-dividing stone (*namiwake-ishi*) and at left a current-dividing stone (*mizuwake-ishi*). Beyond each of these is a larger stone of similar coloring and shape, an unusual technique not often found even in gardens made in olden times.

NISHI HONGANJI TEMPLE, DAISHOIN GARDEN

This was the most extravagant garden of the late sixteenth century and remains striking even today. The main features are the triad of rocks (*sanzon-seki*) that form the dry waterfall (*kare-taki*) at the rear, and the auspiciously symbolic crane and tortoise islands linked by a massive cut-stone bridge. The great wing stone of the crane (middle left), the shape of which also evokes the mountains of the immortals, is a particularly fine example and is reminiscent of other rock arrangements: one in front of Ashiwara island at the Kinkaku pavilion of Rokuonji temple, and the other in the garden of the old Shurinji temple in Kutsuki (Shiga prefecture)—all impressive reminders of the continuity of Japanese garden tradition. It appears that the designers, in constructing the dry falls here, referred to the tradition represented by the dry waterfall of the ancient Tenryuji temple garden and incorporated it into their layout. This is among the few orthodox gardens that form the backbone of Japan's landscape garden tradition. (The trees wrapped in straw against the cold are cycads.)

NISHI HONGANJI TEMPLE, TEKISUIEN GARDEN

Over the bamboo fence rises the Hiunkaku pavilion, designated a National Treasure. Along with the Kinkaku and Ginkaku, this three-tiered shingled-roof structure counts among the "three great pavilions" of Kyoto. From the top level, one can see out over most of the city and the surrounding landscape. The view of Mt. Hiei, in particular, gives one a taste of how it must feel to be "liege of all one beholds." Originally accessible only by boat across the pond, the Hiunkaku can be reached today via the large cut-stone bridge, similar to that in the Daishoin garden (p. 36), connecting the little promontory near the pavilion to the opposite shore. It is said that in olden times the bottom of the pond was paved with round stones, which must have given it a more formally designed appearance.

SHIN'NYOIN TEMPLE GARDEN

While closely resembling an illustration in an eighteenth-century guidebook to famous places and gardens in Kyoto called *Miyako rinsen meisho zue*, the present garden is actually a restoration by Shigemori Mirei (1896–1975) made after World War II. The shrubbery is kept toward the back and the stone arrangements along the dry stream are minimal, accentuating the undulating lines of the moss-covered banks and the stream itself. The flat stones depicting the flow of water partly overlap like fish scales, the effect being quite different depending on whether the stream is viewed from the left or the right. When seen from the reverse end the current seems rapid, rising up in spits and sprays, but from the other direction it looks gentle, flowing smoothly along. This garden has an ornamental quality not often seen in a Japanese garden, a design reminiscent of the taste of Furuta Oribe. The oddly shaped "pear" (*urizane*) lantern is also depicted in *Miyako rinsen meisho zue* and shows how faithfully this garden retains its original appearance.

KANJIIN TEMPLE, SHOIN SOUTH GARDEN

This garden is noted in *Tsukiyama teizoden* (part I), an eighteenth-century garden manual, for the "continuity of its standing stones and shrubbery joined one to another like large beads on a string." The stone bridge across the top of the waterfall is an element seen also in the Ninomaru garden at Nagoya Castle, and the vertical stone cluster to the right of the falls is similar to arrangements found in the Nishi Honganji Daishoin garden (p. 36) and the Sanpoin temple garden, commissioned by the sixteenth-century warlord Toyotomi Hideyoshi. These resemblances lend credence to the temple tradition attributing this design to Kato Kiyomasa, another warlord who was Hideyoshi's contemporary.

REITOIN TEMPLE, SHOIN GARDEN

A solemn hush permeates this temple, an established training hall for Zen meditation. Even without knowing the nature of the temple in advance, one is immediately struck by the atmosphere within its gates, intimating that it should be approached in a serious, reverent frame of mind.

The original pond garden was so highly regarded that it was introduced in *Miyako rinsen meisho zue*, the guidebook to Kyoto mentioned on p. 38. Neglected in later years, it was rebuilt by Shigemori Mirei in the mid-twentieth century. Its highlights include the bridge-supporting stone (*hashizoe-ishi*) at the head of the cut-stone bridge and the large Horai stone doubling as a shore support on the opposite bank.

Kyushoin temple garden

Beyond the hedges of this contemplative pond garden are the roof of the Boketsuro gate of Ken'ninji temple and the hills of Higashiyama. The straight horizontal lines of the two-tiered hedges pull smartly into focus the formal elements set within naturalistic surroundings. Whereas round hedges have only one surface, a rectangular hedge requires trimming on six sides, counting the bottom, considerably increasing the work required for its maintenance. Despite the extra labor, though, straight lines are deliberately preferred here, in order to make the hedges stand out against the contours of Higashiyama and to set off the ridgeline of the Boketsuro gate. The double-hedge technique is the same at that used in the Hojo east garden of Daitokuji temple (p. 24) to incorporate the view of Mt. Hiei.

Ryosokuin temple, Hojo and Shoin east garden

Extending along the east side of the Hojo and Shoin buildings, which stand next to each other on a north-south axis, this long, narrow garden centers on a pond shaped like the Chinese character for "water" (水). A pair of lanterns face each other across the pond. Visible on the far shore are two tea-houses, the Rinchitei on the right and the Suigetsutei on the left. Said to have been designed by Chikushin Jochi (1678–1745), fifth-generation head of the Yabunouchi tea school, this garden simultaneously serves as a strolling pond garden for both Shoin and Hojo and as a tea garden for the tea-houses opposite.

SHODEN EIGEN'IN TEMPLE GARDEN

The name of this temple derives from two temples, Eigen'an and Shoden'in, that later merged together. Shoden'in was the retirement retreat of Oda Urakusai (1547–1621; also known as Joan Uraku), warlord, tea master, and brother of Oda Nobunaga. His tearoom, named Joan, was recently reconstructed (off the photograph, to the right), and although the pond garden does not date back to medieval times either, it is attractively trim and well appointed. Low-lying Chinese juniper spreads a broad carpet of greenery on the right-hand side. The railing in the foreground provides a frame through which one can gaze at the scene with a certain detachment, slightly removed from the context of the garden within. A railing invariably adds a touch of serenity and elegance.

SAIRAIIN TEMPLE GARDEN

A relaxed garden with minimal trace of artifice, too, has its attractions. A hedge of *satsuki* azaleas (Rhododendron indicum) planted along a veranda in this way not only prevents any mud from splashing up onto the veranda when it rains, but serves as ground cover along places where moss does not grow well. The hedge also conceals the drop-off from the veranda, giving the viewer inside the illusion of gazing down on the scene from another, higher dimension. This provides a kind of frame similar to the effect produced by the giant hedge in front of the Rin'untei teahouse at Shugakuin Detached Palace (p. 8).

KIYOMIZUDERA JOJUIN TEMPLE, SHOIN NORTH GARDEN

With its water reaching up close to the Shoin and fanning out as if to enclose it on both sides, the pond seems larger than it is in reality. The triangular shape exploits the laws of perspective to accentuate the illusion of breadth. Behind the hedge is a gully, which, though invisible from the Shoin, makes the "borrowed" scenery of Otowa hill beyond loom closer. Barely visible on the tree-covered slope of the hill, a stone lantern paired with the "Kagero" (mayfly) lantern in the pond further integrates the scenery. The oddly shaped stone to the right of the Kagero lantern is known as the "Eboshi rock" for its similarity to the *eboshi* caps worn by members of the ancient Japanese court, and the small legless stone lantern (*oki doro*) on the far right of the photo is called "Temari" (handball).

KIYOMIZUDERA JOJUIN TEMPLE, SHOIN NORTH GARDEN

This large water basin, of a type placed for use at the edge of a veranda, is named for its resemblance to the long sleeve of a *furisode* kimono. It also looks a little like a sachet bound in the middle with string, for which it has an alternate designation: *tagasode*. Literally meaning "Whose sleeves?" *tagasode* is an allusion to a poem in the medieval *Kokinshu* anthology that goes, "Whose sleeves have brushed the plum blossom and captured its scent so sweet?" It is an elegant name, and a plum tree standing beside a basin of this sort would indeed suit it well.

Ryogin'an temple, Hojo east garden

This garden depicts an episode in the childhood of Daimin Kokushi (third abbot of Tofukuji temple, of which this building is a part), according to which two dogs were said to have defended him from attack by wolves while he lay suffering from a fever. The three stones in the immediate foreground as well as the three seen against the bamboo fence represent the wolves. Of the remaining stones in the center, the one lying flat in the middle represents the child and the two on either side of it are the dogs. In order to meet the challenge of designing a garden to be viewed from three of its four sides, the wolf stones are set at a slant and form a kind of spiral, taking advantage of the fact that a circle faces the front from any direction. The reddish brown gravel is made of "rust gravel" (*sabi jari*) produced in Kurama, on the outskirts of Kyoto.

YOGEN'IN TEMPLE GARDEN

This temple was built by Lady Yodo, consort of Toyotomi Hideyoshi, in memory of her father. Though later damaged by fire, it was rebuilt by Yodo's younger sister, the wife of second Shogun Tokugawa Hidetada, at which time several structures were transported here from the castle at Fushimi, Hideyoshi's last residence, to be used as the main hall and living quarters. Kobori Enshu's extended service as a public works commissioner at Fushimi Castle may explain why the pond garden has been long attributed to his hand. The present-day garden features a waterfall rock arrangement that, in the traditional typology of "masculine" or "feminine" cascades, would be classified as feminine. Stones with flat, level tops descend stepwise along the right side of the large standing stone, suggesting the various stages of a cascade. This pattern of waterfall may also be seen in older gardens, such as the one in the Asakura ruins at Ichijodani (Fukui prefecture) or that of the Daisen'in temple (Kyoto), and leaves no doubt that the builder was well versed in the traditions of Japanese garden design.

YOGEN'IN TEMPLE GARDEN

With the embankment stones kept low and level, one's gaze passes smoothly over the quiet scene of the pond, uninterrupted by any upright rocks. The stone bridge, rather thin in accordance with the preferred taste of Muromachi times, fits in well with the atmosphere evoked by the shoreline. To display brilliant foliage in the autumn, trees need to have plenty of water during the summer; in that regard, the Japanese maples (Acer japonicum) planted near the pond enjoy a favorable environment.

SAISHOIN TEMPLE, KYAKUDEN FOREGARDEN

This is the garden of the guest hall of Saishoin, one of the two temples within the Byodoin temple complex. Laid out in front of a chapel dedicated to the deity Fudo (right center), the garden is of relatively recent design, but makes use of some old garden stones. To the right of the covered well is a Chinese camellia (*to tsubaki*); although still slender, the tree is said to be seventy or eighty years old. The boat-shaped water basin at the edge of the veranda (far right), made by cutting the top off a natural stone and hollowing it out, is an unusual item.

SHOKOKUJI TEMPLE, KAISANDO SOUTH GARDEN

The southeast corner (above) shows the gravel-covered *karesansui* demarcated by its stone curb frame and the corner where the "dragon stream" winds around behind it.

◄ **SHOKOKUJI TEMPLE, KAISANDO SOUTH GARDEN**

Displaying an unusual design combining a gravel-covered *karesansui* expanse surrounded by a frame of stone curbing (*kazura-ishi*) with a dry landscape stream snaking along behind it, this garden is situated on the south side of the hall where the Zen master Muso Soseki (1275–1351) is enshrined. Water used to flow along the now empty streambed once called the "dragon stream," no doubt because of its twisting course. The *karesansui* part of the garden is thought to have been made in the mid-eighteenth century. The eight stones seem to have been distributed over the gravel expanse more or less independently, rather than placed in a closely coordinated arrangement, giving the layout an open, straight-forward quality that could easily be mistaken for something much more modern. The beauty of this garden is more that of its open spaces than the configuration of its stones.

ZUISHUN'IN TEMPLE, HONDO NORTH GARDEN

In this garden, spring unfolds with the yellow flowering of the Japanese cornel dogwood (Cornus officinalis) and the pink of the weeping cherry. Across the pond from the main hall is the Kyushoan teahouse, modeled after the Omote Senke Fushin'an teahouse, with its name inscribed in the gable. The stone-paved path from the main hall branches left onto stepping stones, then crosses the stone bridge with its bamboo railing to the waiting bench beyond the trees. A water basin along the way is equipped with a drain that echoes in a pleasantly musical way (*suikin-kutsu*).

DAIKOMYOJI TEMPLE, HONDO GARDEN

Delicate Chinese bellflowers might seem out of place in a sternly formal *karesansui* garden of white gravel, moss, and stones, but in fact they look perfect here. The choice of flowers for a Japanese garden is quite difficult. Blossoms that are too profuse or colorful can detract from the garden's serenity; the height at which they grow must be appropriate; and they cannot be allowed to just sprout up and spread anywhere. On these points, the *kikyo*, with its pale purple flowers, medium height, and contained perennial growth, is an excellent match. Other flowers that fulfill these conditions are *hagi* (bush clover; Lespedeza), *ominaeshi* (valerian; Valerianaceae), *tsuwabuki* (green leopard plant; Farfugium japonicum), *shukaido* (hardy begonia; Begonia grandis), and *shumeigiku* (Anemone japonica).

JISHOIN TEMPLE, HONDO FOREGARDEN

The azalea (*Kirishima tsutsuji*; Rhododendron obtusum) in full bloom, the new buds of the pine rising vigorously skyward, and the lush growth of haircap moss (*sugi goke*; Polytrichum juniperium) are testimony to constant care. The moss must be meticulously cleaned and the pine tree requires bud-thinning in the spring and tidying of its needles in the fall. The delicate Kirishima azalea is a variety that goes copiously to seed and can sap its own strength if the wilted flowers are not removed early after blooming. A garden gives us beautiful scenes such as this only in return for assiduous care proper to each season and to each plant within it.

JISHOIN TEMPLE, SHOIN FOREGARDEN

The camellia is well loved for its modest elegance. The *wabisuke* variety, with its small flowers and red-white variegation, is particularly favored for a colorful yet quiet beauty that makes it the perfect broadleaf evergreen for a garden. There are many deciduous flowering trees, like the popular plum and cherry, but camellias are among the few broadleaf evergreens with attractive flowers, and they look lovely even after they have fallen on the ground. The water basin here is an oval-shaped cavity in the top of a rectangular column of stone. This shape makes the basin easier to extract water from and simpler to clean than if it had been a regular rectangle.

DAISHOJI TEMPLE, HONDO GARDEN

Known as the "Temple Palace," Daishoji was a convent where women of imperial or aristocratic blood lived after retiring from the court and becoming nuns. Running through this garden in front of the main hall is a long, narrow dry-landscape pond lined with round stones. It curves gently down the gradual slope with the grace of a quiet brook flowing through an open field. The straight and arched bridges and the rock arrangements blend inconspicuously into the scene. The beds of moss where temple inhabitants might pick wildflowers or stretch out a mat to brew tea out of doors, together with the stone lantern and the red pine —all are positioned with skillfully calculated casualness. This is a garden that aspires in every respect to the ideal of the natural, as if the very act of contrivance were in poor taste.

Daishoji temple, Shoin garden

Abloom with hollyhocks and bush clover, this is a gentle, easygoing garden. Gardens with flowering shrubs are difficult to organize. Designed for the pleasure of those who want to enjoy flowers at close quarters, they are filled with plants of low or medium height, at the inevitable expense of orderliness. For varieties that bloom well only with plenty of sunlight, particularly like these hollyhocks, trees and shrubs that cast shade from above must be kept to a minimum. The remedy found here is a couple of red pines and a stone lantern that anchor the design, with the flowers grouped in ripples around them. A similar combination of red pine and lantern may be found in the design of the garden of the main hall.

SANJI CHIONJI TEMPLE GARDEN

The garden of the living quarters of this imperial convent, nicknamed the "Irie Palace," is known as the "garden of the immortals" (Horai no niwa). A shallow dry-landscape pond is spread with white gravel, a stone bridge dividing the pond in two. Shallow though it may be, crossing over the water via a bridge symbolizes passing from this world to the Pure Land, an arcadia difficult to reach. The large stone just to the left beyond the bridge is the Horai stone.

The unusual name of the temple, "Three Prayer Hours," apparently refers to the practice there of reciting sutras and prayers three times a day instead of the six prayer times day and night observed at the imperial palace.

HONKOIN TEMPLE GARDEN

Recognizing the crane-tortoise stones in a garden can heighten one's enjoyment of it; and since the crane stones tend to be comparatively abstract, it helps to look for the tortoise first. Here, to the left of the small pine on the far right of the photograph, a tortoise's head can be seen poking out between two blocks of stone. Another lies beyond the natural stone bridge, projecting to the left out of the slope of the artificial hill. And beyond, in the center, flanking a dry waterfall, are the wings of the crane. This dynamic design is characteristic of the early seventeenth century.

Hokyoji temple, Hondo south garden

While autumn leaves glinting in the sun are certainly beautiful, the view from underneath the canopy is equally engaging: through the tinted transparency of the foliage one feels drawn into the light of the sky beyond. Old maples such as those in this garden shed unnecessary branches naturally over time, and gardeners, in fact, look to these ancient trees as models for thinning branches to best effect. When an ideal amount of space is left between them, a fine tracery results.

◀ Hokyoji temple, Hondo north garden

Beyond the bridge, rocks crowd up to the left and right of the path as if in pursuit of the stepping stones, reminding one of a passage in *Sakuteiki* about "stones that flee and stones that pursue." Since it is known as a "crane-tortoise garden," the large stone protruding at an angle at the crest of the hill may be assumed to be the head of the tortoise; and though not visible in this photograph, a stone arrangement buttressing the bank of the *karesansui* pond at the foot of the artificial hill is probably the crane. The backdrop of a bamboo grove heightens the brilliance of the autumn foliage.

KOSHOIN TEMPLE, SHOIN NORTH GARDEN

A pair of Japanese white pines, one five hundred and the other three hundred years old, flourish companionably in this elegant garden on the north side of the Shoin of this imperial convent known as the "Tokiwa Gosho" (Palace of Eternity). These great trees, planted and cultivated by generations of abbesses, are quiet testimony to Koshoin's long history. At the back on the far right stands a five-layer stupa with the name of the Amida Nyorai buddha inscribed in Sanskrit, while a treasure ship heads for harbor on the sea of white gravel stretching before it.

KOSEIJI TEMPLE GARDEN

The moss-covered hillocks of this garden, called Shinwatei, trace the character for "heart" (心; taken from the temple's alternate name of Shin-wazan) in bold brushstrokes sweeping across the white gravel. The swirl patterns drawn in the gravel emulate the watermarks in the "paper." As if in calligraphic relief, the rocks project the character's shape, one stone at an angle at the far left for the first stroke; seven stones for the second stroke, a long sweeping line; two stones for the third, a stroke toward the top right; and two stones diagonally below them for the fourth and final stroke. The patterns in the gravel are characteristic of Shigemori Mirei's distinctive design approach, as is the bamboo fence on the right featuring an abstract pattern of the same brushstrokes.

KOSEIJI TEMPLE, KURI FOREGARDEN

Passing along the stone pavement inside the front gate of the temple brings one to this arrangement of rocks built directly in front of the Kuri (monks' quarters) some years after the Shinwatei garden with its brushstroke design (previous page), which lies further along the path to the left. The peak of the huge central stone is aligned with the gable of the building. The other stones cluster around the central one to form the shape of Mt. Shumisen, a mythical mountain in Buddhist cosmology. Perhaps the most distinctive feature is the raised expanse of swirl-raked sand, forming a sort of beachhead around the central arrangement. Located on the spot where an ancient pine once stood, this garden was created as a kind of prayer for the repose of the spirit of the tree.

Seirenji temple, Kyakuden south garden

The view of the south garden from the guest quarters extends to the chapel to Jizo at the right side. Led by the standing stones flanking the lantern, the others in the garden move toward the chapel in radiating lines as though Jizo—the bodhisattva revered as the guardian of children—were drawing them toward his faith. The stone triad at the top of the artificial hill faces directly toward the guest quarters, solid symbols of the ideal world. The design is by the author.

JOTOKUIN TEMPLE, KURI SOUTH GARDEN

This grouping is meant to evoke the Buddha and bodhisattvas riding on a cloud, coming to welcome souls to Paradise. The plantings include Japanese maple, pink plum, and linden (Tilia miqueliana Maxim.). The photo at left shows a tea garden set apart in the left corner of the garden pictured above by a bamboo lattice fence. It consists of a simple hand-washing place and basin front stone (*mae-ishi*) accompanied by a black pine. The moss-covered bank has a checkerboard pattern of small paving stones. The design is by the author.

NAN'YOIN TEMPLE, HONDO SOUTH GARDEN

The simplicity of this flat *karesansui* garden, featuring only three large stones, is surprising given the lavishly appointed country villa gardens for which designer Ogawa Jihei (1860–1933) is known; but the temple to which it belongs was founded in 1903 by the Zen priest Dokutan, one of whose seven precepts for living was, "Be not ostentatious in dress or diet." Though a *karesansui*, it is bright and open, with the modern flair characteristic of Ogawa's works, incorporating into the entire prospect the landscape beyond the low hedge at the back.

Nan'yoin Temple Garden

On the other side of this pond garden may be seen the main hall, with the garden shown on the previous page lying beyond. The key to a successful pond garden is the water supply: the water must be plentiful, pure, and low in temperature, with drainage at the lower end. This garden, like many in this part of Kyoto, draws on the Lake Biwa Canal as a resource. The "snow-viewing" lantern fits in well with the pond, perhaps because the horizontal spread of its broad roof echoes the sprawling lines of the shore.

Konkai Komyoji temple garden

A spacious landscape garden spreads out in the area bounded by the Daihojo hall in the background, the Shiuntei teahouse on the right, and the living quarters on the left. When different buildings share the same garden as here, a point of particular interest is how the garden is arranged with respect to each, as mentioned with regard to the Omote Senke garden (p. 11). A meandering stream has been dug in the area midway between the azalea hedge and the Daihojo to coordinate it with the pond garden off to the right (shown on the next page). Pine trees behind the teahouse, their branches upstretched like the wings of a crane, form a subtle division between the stream area and the other parts of the garden. Techniques such as these make it possible to achieve a unified design despite the orientation of the garden in different directions.

KONKAI KOMYOJI TEMPLE GARDEN

This pond garden, equipped with bridges in stroll-garden style, lies just
below the woods visible on the right-hand side of the photograph on the
previous page. The rock arrangement on the left is in the robust style
characteristic of the early seventeenth century. Since the temple was one
of the four leading temples of the Jodo sect, the pond can be assumed to
stand for the Pure Land (Jodo). In autumn the brilliant branches of the
maples reaching out over the pond evoke the luminous cloud on which
the Buddha is said to appear to carry souls off to Paradise.

Eishoin temple, Shoin foregarden

Taking advantage of the depth afforded by constructing it against the edge of the hill at its back, this garden faces the Shoin of Eishoin, a subtemple of Konkai Komyoji. The creation of a pond at the foot of the hill where rainwater naturally collects is another gardening technique making good use of the topography. The *karesansui* garden in the foreground is of recent design. The gravel-covered area extending back on the left-hand side and spanned by a stone bridge is in the image of a waterfall flowing out of the hills. The stepping stones in the right foreground lead from the Shoin to the "Myojo" (morning star) well which is counted among the eight sights of the Kurodani area occupied by the temple complex. A bodhisattva is said to have appeared after the morning star fell into the water of this well.

REIKANJI TEMPLE GARDEN

This view from the Shoin east garden takes in the main hall of an imperial convent belonging to the Rinzai Zen sect and the covered corridor at left connecting it to the Shoin lower down on the hill. The steep bank has been turned into a hill garden, with the stones arranged not merely as an embankment but as compositional elements in a design that includes a "snow-viewing" lantern. As in the case of this slope, it is often wiser to design around difficult natural conditions than to attempt to alter them. The brilliant foliage of the Japanese maple makes a striking contrast with the green of the red pine. There is nothing exotic about these or the other trees at this temple, including the camellias that flourish here; indeed, it may be that trees best suited to the local soil and climate are the most aesthetically appealing.

HONEN'IN TEMPLE, HOJO GARDEN

Honen'in was originally founded by the priest Honen (1132–1212) and rebuilt in the seventeenth century by Banbu, the thirty-eighth abbot of Chion'in temple, as a center for spiritual training. From the Hojo, the bulging promontory on the opposite side looks like an island in the pond. A stone bridge connects this promontory to a point of land on the Hojo side. This composition, though smaller in scale, is similar to the "Pure Land" style (*jodo-shiki*) gardens at Byodoin and Joruriji temples. The bridge represents the crossing from this world to Paradise on the other side.

HONEN'IN TEMPLE, HOJO GARDEN

This photo, taken from the promontory featured on the previous page, shows a view of the Hojo under a veil of maple leaves. This hill-and-pond garden lies at the foot of Zenkisan, the hill that gives the temple its alternate name. A natural spring with its source higher up fills the pond with crystal clear water. In the cool, clean air flowing from deep in the hills, the maples, moss, rocks—everything glows with verdant vigor.

Keitokuin temple, Hondo garden

Cool, pure water from deep in the mountains flows over a waterfall into this garden created for a temple in the northeastern outskirts of Kyoto belonging to the Rinzai Zen sect. The sharp-edged rocks of the local Ohara area give the arrangements a rugged strength. This garden shows the kind of solid artistry rarely seen in newly designed gardens today; it is an ambitious work devoted to the pursuit of beauty in the arrangement of stones. The old Shurinji temple garden at Kutsuki (in Shiga prefecture) served as a model for it, and traces of its influence may be seen in the form of the stream-like pond, shaped like the character for "heart" (心). A five-hundred-year-old wild cherry (Prunus jamasakura) and a Japanese maple standing on the opposite shore assure the garden a special glory in both spring and autumn.

TOKAIAN TEMPLE *TSUBONIWA* (ENCLOSED GARDEN)

Verandas surround this rectangular garden. Three rocks in the foreground and three in the back are arranged symmetrically with the stone in the center as the pivot. The smallest stone of the front group is positioned slightly to one side, directing one's gaze toward the right, while the smallest stone of the back group is shifted to the left in order to draw one's attention in that direction. The center stone balances the two groups like a pair of scales, giving the garden both tension and focus. The pattern in the gravel is of ripples moving continuously outward from the center stone, encompassing all the arrangements and uniting them into a coherent whole.

TOKAIAN TEMPLE, HOJO SOUTH GARDEN

This garden, with neither tree nor shrub disturbing the tranquil lines raked into white gravel, adheres to the form prescribed by the true function of a Hojo south garden as a space reserved for ceremony and ritual. A proper garden had to be sacred and pure in conformity with its original purpose as a place for feeling the presence of the spiritual and invoking it in this world. The expanse of white gravel with its pattern of straight lines betraying not a hint of worldly doubt is the ultimate representation of a spiritual realm far removed from the mundane. This is no place for the unenlightened.

TOKAIAN TEMPLE, SHOIN GARDEN

The garden manual *Tsukiyama senjiroku* by the Zen priest Toboku records that its author created this flat dry landscape garden sometime in the Bunka era (1804–1818). Three large standing stones in the back grouped close together in a Buddhist triad (*sanzon*) provide the focus of the garden, while a flat pedestal stone lying at their foot lends stability to the arrangement. The triad also doubles as a waterfall, with the pedestal serving as the "cascade-receiving" stone (*mizuuke-ishi*) at its base and the flat stone in front of it as the "current-dividing" stone (*mizuwake-ishi*) separating the water into two streams. An elongated water basin stands next to the veranda at lower right. The large flat slab beside it is called a prayer stone.

GYOKUHOIN TEMPLE GARDEN

Stepping stones made of large natural slabs connect the Fusuisen well and the Gyokuhoin-style water basin sitting on a lotus leaf-shaped pedestal. The path comes to an end at the Shoun'in, a chapel in memory of Toyotomi Hideyoshi's first son Sutemaru, who died in infancy. To the left (not pictured) is a shrine to retired Emperor Hanazono, whose former detached palace grounds were dedicated to the temple, and to the right is another enshrining Kanzan Egen, the temple's founder. There is a distinct spiritual atmosphere in this courtyard bounded by these memorial structures. The visitor must first wash using the "dew" filling the lotus-footed basin, and then draw holy water from the well as an offering to Buddha. The well is sacred, too, since it marks the site where the founder is said to have passed away after leaving the temple in the care of his successor.

GYOKUHOIN TEMPLE GARDEN

This part of the garden is notable for its bold stone arrangements. The arrangements, however, do not face any of the buildings surrounding the garden; instead they are turned in the direction of the Fusuisen well, said to be the site of the temple founder's death. The garden is not intended for appreciation or for strolling in, or for any other purpose save to venerate the well. It is likely that the latter was once surrounded by neither stepping stones nor moss but an expanse of white gravel similar to that in the south garden (though practical considerations may have led to the use of moss in the area around the stone arrangements). Such a composition would perhaps have better suited the mystical associations of the well, besides giving the garden a more unified appearance.

SAIHOJI TEMPLE, DRY LANDSCAPE

One cannot help but admire the dynamics of this dry landscape in the Saihoji upper garden. Though seemingly placed at random, the masterful combination of even and uneven contours reveals the composition to have been calculated with a subtlety that defies imitation. The design consists of three clusters of rocks placed in descending steps, each separated by a small plateau of open ground. Though these empty spaces are not visible from below, so that all three series of steps appear as one, their presence sets off the rock formations to stronger effect, in much the same way that distant "borrowed" scenery is set off by a garden.

SAIHOJI TEMPLE, POND GARDEN

The round tortoise-shaped pond has two large islands in its center located back to back, accompanied by smaller islands and rocky outcrops clustered concentrically, while a path encircles the pond in such a way that the viewer's attention is constantly directed toward the center. The rise and fall of perspective brought about by changes in elevation becomes particularly pronounced as the path approaches the climactic vantage point, adding complexity to the effect. Over the centuries moss has grown on the soil among the cobblestones lining the embankment to create a luxuriant surface. It is as if time itself has enveloped the banks of the pond, filling the garden with the ethereal light of an otherworldly realm.

SHOGAKUJI TEMPLE GARDEN

Shogakuji, hidden quietly away to the north of Nonomiyajinja shrine in Kyoto's Saga district, offers one of the best views of Mt. Arashiyama. Nothing clamors for attention in this simple garden composed only of a water basin and dry pond, where time passes at the relaxed pace of the city's suburbs. The foliage is vibrant with color and haircap moss grows in abundance, no doubt because Saga is much colder in the mornings and evenings compared to the heart of the city and also gets thick morning mists. In order for it to flourish, haircap moss requires adequate sunlight, plenty of moisture and air, as well as diligent weeding and cleaning.

ENRIAN TEMPLE GARDEN

Enrian stands in an elegant locale said to have once been a retreat owned by the famed poet Fujiwara no Teika (1162–1241). A spreading maple and an Oribe-style lantern accompany a water basin beside the hedge on the left side of the Shoin south garden pictured here. The right side, containing nothing but a lush carpet of moss, indulges in the luxury of empty space. A path extends from the inner gate at the far left, but the stepping stones leading from the Shoin do not join it, instead coming to an abrupt end halfway. One's gaze hovers expectantly over this lovely spot before noting with a small shock that there is no other destination. It is a case where the absence of something expected paradoxically succeeds in giving it overwhelming presence.

SANSHUIN TEMPLE TEA GARDEN

The open structure of the wicket gate and lattice fence allows the viewer's gaze to slip freely to and fro to encompass the entire garden. The fence has been simplified, with only three crossbars of bamboo where there usually would be four. This view must be of the outer garden, since a wicket gate typically opens inward. The long stones set in a raft pattern cleverly combine a sharp turn of the path with a branch off to another part of the garden.

DONGEIN TEMPLE GARDEN

The name of this imperial convent comes from *udumbara*, Sanskrit for a mythical flower said to bloom once every three thousand years. Plantings pushed into the background surround the broad expanse of moss in front. The tranquil greenery enfolds the viewer in a soothing embrace that contrasts with the stern formality of the white gravel space found in the Tokaian Hojo south garden (p. 82). Though a low hill has been constructed in the right center, complete with some stones arranged along its foot, these remain small and inconspicuous compared to the garden's size. The open spaciousness of the garden seems intended to make the viewer feel as if afloat within nature's green womb.

Yoshiminedera temple, Hondo garden

Brilliantly colored carp swim in a pond crossed by bridges and surrounded by lanterns and stone arrangements. There is nothing spectacular about this prototypically Japanese garden, but its serenity affords a comforting welcome to the pilgrim wearied by the long, steep climb to the temple. The famed "gamboling dragons pine" (*yuryumatsu*), a Japanese white pine said to be over three hundred years old, also flourishes within the temple grounds.

Okazaki Tsuruya, stone path

*Kyoto's gardens showcase the complexions of each
season, one to the next, from camellias brightening
late-winter shrubbery to cherry blossoms and
fresh green leaves parading in spring; from rain-
drenched hydrangea and cool pools of lotus in
summer to bush clover and bright foliage in
autumn; and thence back to winter's still blankets of
white. Their forms are equally diverse, from vast
villa landscapes to miniature courtyards. For
over a thousand years this land of pleasant
hills and pristine rivers has left a legacy of
countless beautiful gardens.*

TAIRYU SANSO VILLA GARDEN

The completion of the Lake Biwa Canal in 1890 led to the creation of numerous villa gardens in the Nanzenji area to its east. Gardeners drew on its abundant supply of water to make ponds and streams, with "borrowed" scenery from the lovely Higashiyama hills in the background. Possession of a villa garden of this sort soon became a status symbol for the wealthy. Instrumental in setting this trend in motion was Ogawa Jihei (p. 72), also known by his professional name Ueji. He designed almost all of these gardens, including those at Tairyu Sanso, Murin'an, the Sumitomo villa, Seifuso (pp. 96–97), and Seiryutei (pp. 98–99). The Tairyu Sanso garden is intended for strolling in and incorporates both pond and stream styles. The pond has a central island and several rocky islets, while its stone arrangements, composed mainly of horizontal and recumbent rocks, remain rather unassuming. Perhaps reflecting the cultural trend of the times, the stone arrangements in this and other local villa gardens do not call out for attention but blend into the naturalistic design of the garden.

SEIFUSO VILLA GARDEN

This garden made by Ogawa Jihei was owned by the Meiji era statesman Saionji Kinmochi (1849–1940). The long, shallow pond gives easy access to the water, and the grass carpeting its banks and island lends the open space a sunny quality quite unlike that pertaining to moss. Moss is uninviting and otherworldly; grass is more practical and friendly. Beyond the lawn, a stand of shapely red pines gives way to the woods in the background. Rising above them is Nyoigadake, with a direct view of the outline of the character 大 (*dai*; "big") etched on the hillside. Along this outline, farewell fires are lit to the spirits that are believed to visit during the Obon festival in midsummer.

SEIRYUTEI OUTER TEA GARDEN

An S-shaped curve of paving stones set in the *arare-koboshi* pattern leads to the garden's inner gate. Inside the gate is the Shirasagi tearoom, pictured on the next page. The path continues past the gate to a waiting bench behind which is a *setchin* (privy), all discreetly concealed by the Japanese pieris hedges to the right until one is nearly upon them. On the left side, too, a stand of *hisakaki* trees (Eurya japonica) planted atop a gentle moss-covered slope keeps the Shoin behind from view. This is a garden that does not reveal all, but makes one bide one's time.

SEIRYUTEI INNER TEA GARDEN

Looking toward the inner gate from the crawl-in entrance of the Shirasagi tearoom shows the stepping stones from the gate. Another stone path leads, in one direction, to the villa's main entrance, and in the other to a water basin. Had these routes traced straight lines, they would have joined in a cross near the center of the garden, but since this formation is disfavored, two small stones have been placed at the intersection, breaking the regularity of the pattern. Although Ogawa's gardens are noted for their boldness and grandeur, this one shows that he was also capable of attentiveness to the finer details.

OKAZAKI TSURUYA GARDEN

Tsuruya, one of Kyoto's most elegant restaurants, maintains a garden of equally high standards. The arched stone bridge with balustrades imparts a classic dignity to the landscape, and all the stones used, whether for aesthetic or utilitarian purposes, have been selected with great care. Created in the early twentieth century by Kato Kumakichi, the garden was originally part of a villa owned by the Nomura family, who presided over a financial conglomerate active in the Kansai area. Ownership passed to

Tsuruya in 1928, and though a large hall built by distinguished modern architect Yoshida Isoya was later added in 1964, the garden was left largely undisturbed. The photograph here is of the east garden as seen from the first floor (called the "Fuku no ma" room, sixty-two mats in size) of the hall. The stylish railing along its two-meter wide tatami-floored veranda and the blinds hung above together form a perfect frame for the garden.

OKAZAKI TSURUYA GARDEN

A large temple foundation stone at lower left marks a dividing point in the path, which continues on to the right as far as the large hall pictured on the previous page. Beyond the arched bridge is a moss-covered rise and a rest house where the viewer may pause to spend a quiet moment gazing out over the garden listening to the sound of the stream. Impressively shaped crags of rock jut out here and there along the stream, seeming to enhance the clarity of the water flowing by. The evergreens in the background have been deliberately chosen for their somber hue, reflect-

ing the designer's conception of this garden as a sort of generously sized tea garden with the rest house serving as a waiting area. Kato regarded tea gardens as his real forte and this one may thus be seen as testifying to his pride in his art. It is a masterpiece built by a man who sought to preserve the spiritual traditions of the Japanese garden at a time, around the turn of the twentieth century, when the more fashionable villa gardens were becoming increasingly popular among the elite.

RAKUSUI GARDEN

Rakusui is an inn famed for its Kyoto cuisine as well as for its garden designed by Ogawa Jihei in 1909. The elongated pond shaped like Lake Biwa is crossed by three bridges that are connected by a path meandering through the garden. (The third bridge, made of natural blue stone, cannot be seen but is located off the bottom of the photograph toward the right.) The highlights of the garden are the stepping stones and long stone bridge in the shallows at the back of the pond; the Gasendo pavilion standing as if afloat on the water; and the backdrop provided by the contours and colors of the Higashiyama hills. The design of Gasendo apparently emulates the Ukimido, a Buddhist chapel located on the waters of Shiga prefecture's real Lake Biwa.

SHIRAKAWAIN GARDEN

Shirakawain, now a boarding facility for private universities, was originally a residence owned by a wealthy kimono merchant . The name derives from a villa owned by the Heian-period regent Fujiwara no Yoshifusa (804–872) which once stood in this area. The garden was laid out by Ogawa Jihei in the early twentieth century. Water from the Lake Biwa Canal is drawn in at the left, flowing over a waterfall to the stepping stones and pond below. The meticulously cared-for red pines are a characteristic element of Ogawa's gardens. The pine for dignity, cherry for passion, and brilliant autumn maples for fleeting beauty: these Ogawa put to use with artistry and taste to adorn fine suburban estates.

SHAKUSUIEN GARDEN

A vast pond garden stretches like a long ribbon along the foothills of Higashiyama from the northwest to the southeast. Though now owned by JT Kyoto Senbai Hospital, this garden originally belonged to Myohoin temple located immediately to the south. The pond has two islands, large and small, with a series of five rocky islets placed in a line near the larger one. This configuration is also seen at Osawanoike pond in Daikakuji temple, and since that garden was made in the Heian era it is thought that Shakusuien, too, may date back to those times. If so, it is likely to be part of the remains of the Komatsu residence owned by Taira no Shigemori (1138–1179), which stood in this area before Myohoin was built. Shigemori was the eldest son of Taira no Kiyomori, head of the famed Heike clan, and it would be no surprise if he had owned a garden as extensive as this one.

KITAMURA MUSEUM, SHIKUNSHIEN GARDEN

The Chinchiriren teahouse, supposedly named from the sound of the samisen, stands in a corner of the Shikunshien garden (literally, "Garden of Four Noblemen"). Visible under the shoji panels set along the top half of the wall in the Kohoan style (pp. 28–29) is a wood-floored veranda that connects with the tearoom. In front of the veranda, water flows out of a bamboo pipe into a basin made from a reliquary encasement stone, spilling over into a sinuous pond. The "snow-viewing" lantern displays an unusual triangular shape. The remarkable works of stone found in Shikunshien are not merely accessories to the beauty of the garden; rather, the garden is expressly designed as a setting where they can be seen to best effect.

KITAMURA MUSEUM, CHINCHIRIREN TEA GARDEN

Slabs of Kurama stone glisten somberly in this garden attached to the Chinchiriren teahouse. The small stone behind and to the left of the humped step-up stone is an example of the *asobi-ishi* (extra-stone) technique. The jewel finial, roof, and lamp housing of the Shokado "patch-work lantern," composed of stones of different origins, are all particularly well balanced. In the aged and weathered atmosphere of this garden, the maples stretching their trunks hesitantly upward add a refreshing breath of youthfulness. An air of nobility pervades the garden.

107

YOMEI BUNKO, KOZANSO SOUTH GARDEN

Yomei Bunko is a private library built by the politician and prime minister Konoe Fumimaro (1891–1945) to house archives passed down through his family, known for its princely heritage. The garden pictured here serves as the foregarden to a tearoom within the library grounds. Cedar and bamboo enclose the back of it, blocking out the sight of the modern city beyond. Although the garden is quite simple, featuring little more than the azaleas and a few stones placed as accents, it has the refinement and unaffected repose appropriate to a villa belonging to an aristocratic family. We can well imagine Fumimaro himself indulging a moment's quiet relaxation on the railed veranda overlooking the garden.

SHIORIAN COURTYARD GARDEN

This courtyard garden belongs to the Kawasaki residence, a prominent example of the *machiya* townhouses of Kyoto. Shiorian is the name of both the tearoom within the residence and the Kawasaki family business. In the foreground lies the study, in the back the storehouse, and to the left a covered walkway. The view of the garden is framed by the branches of the Japanese maple planted at the edge of the veranda, in a technique also employed in the Hiiragiya inn garden (pp. 110–111). The hexagonal stone lantern in the center provides the focus of the garden, with the stepping stones leading up to it having a presence of their own. The large temple foundation stone in the center, the black ornamental stone at center left, the water basin beside the veranda (not visible), and the gray stone where one removes one's shoes were clearly selected with discriminating taste, to create a garden of high caliber. The central black stone, notable for its sheen, is said to represent a tortoise, while a whitish stone situated behind it is a crane. In the life of a merchant family, importance is attached to such symbols of longevity and good fortune.

Hiiragiya courtyard garden

This garden lies in front of the innermost room of the Hiiragiya inn, a highly respected establishment in business since 1818. Spanned by an arched bridge, stepping stones, and another raft-style bridge, a stream murmurs pleasantly through the scenery, providing a place for a variety of water's-edge enjoyments. The spirit of the inn, which is sophisticated without being pretentious and which seeks to make its guests feel more like residents than visitors, permeates the garden as well. Though at first glance quite unremarkable, its tasteful modesty is calm and soothing.

Masuume TSUBONIWA

Though this flat dry landscape garden is quite small, the interplay between the stones—some functional and others ornamental—sharing the same space gives it a feeling of tension and focus. The path starting from the paving at the right and continuing via a round temple foundation stone to the step where one removes one's shoes provides a counterpoint to the pair of rocks closer to the wall. In the left corner, a water basin made of natural stone with a sheered-off top serves to absorb the momentum of the larger rock opposite. The stone immediately to the right of the basin is a flat "water-dipping" stone that serves as a platform for those using the basin.

APPRECIATION
OF A
JAPANESE GARDEN

Masaaki Ono

Japanese gardens may be divided into three types: pond (chisen) gardens, dry landscape (karesansui) gardens, and tea gardens (roji). This essay presents the basic information about the standard features of such gardens needed to appreciate both their beauty and their significance in full.

THE POND GARDEN

Chisen gardens are in three main styles: the pleasure boat (*chisen shuyu-shiki*), stroll (*chisen kaiyu-shiki*), and contemplative (*chisen zakan-shiki*; also called *kansho-shiki*) styles. For convenience, these are discussed separately, but in reality they are often combined. The pleasure boat and stroll styles, or the stroll and contemplative styles, can often be found within a single garden. The focus of appreciation is on whichever style is prominent in a particular garden.

THE PLEASURE BOAT GARDEN

This type of garden design reached its peak in the aristocratic estates established during the Heian period, between the eighth and twelfth centuries. The fashion then was for pairs of boats, the bow of one carved with a dragon's head and the other with the head of a *geki*, to glide along while musicians played in a pavilion on a nearby island. The *geki* is an imaginary, heron-like water bird, said to be able to fly well even in stormy weather and to be a skillful diver. Since the dragon is also said to preside over water, both creatures must have been carved on the bows to ward off possible accidents.

The vantage point of a person sitting in a boat is naturally low, so the landscape looms up powerfully before passing by. Also, unlike someone walking along a garden path where viewpoints are necessarily restricted, the occupant of a moving boat is free to enjoy the scenery from a variety of shifting angles, and to appreciate devices in the design that might otherwise remain unnoticed.

A fine example of a medieval pond garden is Shakusuien (p. 105).

Plan of a Heian-period mansion
(from "Kaoku zakko," *Kojiruien*)

Stream in a Heian mansion garden (from "Nenjugyoji emaki,"
Kojiruien)

THE STROLL GARDEN

The *chisen kaiyu-shiki* garden is meant to be viewed while strolling along paths that circle the pond or cross over to its islands. The garden at Saihoji temple, created during the Kamakura period (1185–1333), is a prominent example (p. 87). While walking is less conducive to the constant shifting of horizontal perspectives afforded by movement over water, the changes in elevation as the path proceeds offer a variety of vantage points not possible from a boat. Indeed, the ascents and descents of the Saihoji garden path are designed very deliberately, with the best vantage point located on high ground and the slope carefully calculated to give the viewer the excitement of proceeding from an overlook of the whole garden to an appreciation of its finer details. The experience of savoring different levels of vertical perspective at every step is part of the enjoyment offered neither by the pleasure boat nor contemplative styles.

Examples of the stroll style created during the Edo period (1603–1868) include imperial gardens such as the Oikeniwa pond garden at Kyoto Imperial Palace (p. 3), the Sento Imperial Palace garden (pp. 4–5), and those of the Katsura (p. 6) and Shugakuin (pp. 8–9) Detached Palaces. During and after the Meiji era (1868–1912), the style was employed in gardens of the country villas of the wealthy including Tairyu Sanso (pp. 94–95) and Seifuso (pp. 96–97), both still privately owned today, as well as the Rakusui inn (pp. 102–103), the Shirakawain hostel (p. 104), and the Okazaki Tsuruya Japanese restaurant (pp. 100–101), which now function as commercial establishments.

THE CONTEMPLATIVE GARDEN

Here, the viewer's gaze remains focused within the garden's boundaries. The pond is enclosed by hedges and by hills both natural and artificial so that all but the *shakkei*, or those parts of the background landscape intentionally "borrowed" for the design, are hidden from view. Aside from the fact that the pond is filled with real water, it is meant to be appreciated very much like the dry landscape garden—in a static way from an adjacent building—and the variety of perspectives offered is admittedly limited in comparison with the pleasure boat or stroll garden styles.

Historically, the pond garden for contemplation arose as a miniaturized adaptation of the dry landscape garden, which was itself derived from the traditional pond garden. Generally compact and vivid in appearance, it was given depth by the same spiritual presence that infused the dry landscape garden, even though designers seem to have found the beauty of water, an element absent in the latter, hard to resist.

The contemplative style continued to develop during and after the Edo era, long after the dry landscape garden had reached its prime. Examples include the Fushimi-Inari Grand Shrine office

Reitoin temple (from *Miyako rinsen meisho zue*)

Shoden'in temple (from *Miyako rinsen meisho zue*), now called Shoden Eigen'in

Kiyomizudera Jojuin temple (from *Miyako rinsen meisho zue*)   Yogen'in temple (from *Miyako rinsen meisho zue*)

garden (p. 19), the gardens at the temples of Hoshun'in (p. 33), Reitoin (pp. 40–41), Kyushoin (p. 42), Ryosokuin (p. 43), Shoden Eigen'in (p. 44), Kiyomizudera Jojuin (pp. 46–48), Yogen'in (pp. 50–51), Nan'yoin (p. 73), Honen'in (pp. 78–79), and Keitokuin (p. 80), the garden of the main hall at Yoshiminedera temple (p. 92), and the Hiiragiya inn garden (pp. 110–111).

Four key elements form the focus for appreciating a pond garden.

OUTLINE AND EMBANKMENT

In viewing a pond garden, attention must be paid first of all to the shape of the pond as well as to the qualities of its shoreline. The *Sakuteiki*, an influential treatise on the art of garden design written during the Heian period, states that "The pond should be dug in the shape of a tortoise or a crane. The water will assume the form of the vessel into which it flows." Examples of a typical tortoise-shaped pond may be seen in the gardens of Saihoji temple (p. 87), Tenryuji temple, and the Kinkaku pavilion at Rokuonji temple. As for the crane shape, the exact form is not defined, but it seems to have referred to a pond constricted in the middle, such as that seen in the Nanzen'in temple garden or the garden at Tenjuan in Nanzenji temple. This precept, however, applied only to the *Sakuteiki*-style garden, and many other types of ponds are to be found, such as the *suiji-ike*, shaped like the character for "water" (水); the *aji-ike*, in the form of the first character of the Sanskrit alphabet; the *shinji-ike*, similar in form to the kanji for "heart" (心); and the *ryuchi* or "dragon pond."

The *Sakuteiki* also notes the aesthetic importance of the contours of the shoreline. After the passage quoted above, it goes on to stipulate that designers should follow the curved shapes of the *hiragana* script rather than the angular lines of Chinese ideographs, and that auspicious words should be their inspiration, the letter *so* (そ) being one such form to emulate. The pebble beaches of the Kyoto and Sento Imperial Palaces both adhere to this precept. But while creating a gently elliptical shoreline may be possible in a garden of sufficient scale for a large pond, the embankment will inevitably become more angular where space is more limited. Thus other techniques have been devised for shaping the contours of ponds, for example by making use of stone arrangements, weirs (*shigarami*), weighted baskets (*jakago*), or stakes.

Stones may be arranged along the whole shore or in particular parts in order to create points of interest. *Shigarami* are bank-reinforcing works made by weaving branches and pieces of bamboo between stakes erected in the pond. With the passage of time the roots of the water plants and surrounding trees stabilize the soil, preventing erosion, so that by the time the branches and bamboo rot away a natural earthen bank has been formed. *Jakago* are baskets made of bamboo or wire filled with cobblestones and piled into several horizontal rows. Here again, the ground grows solid as soil and plant roots fill the spaces between the cobbles. Stakes of stone, concrete, or charred lumber placed at irregular intervals are also used to shore up pond banks.

The aim is ultimately to remove any trace of human artifice. In a garden, the quality of *sabi*—the natural patina and refinement conferred by the passage of time—is an element much to be desired.

ISLANDS AND ROCKY ISLETS

The pond may have only one island or it may have many. There may be a single island representing the legendary Mr. Horai (in Chinese, Penglai), or a pair of islands suggesting a crane and tortoise. In some cases a series of islands may be used to symbolize Horai, Hojo (Fangzhang), Eishu (Yingzhou), and Koryo (Huliang), the four islands said to be the abodes of the immortals. The design of a pond garden becomes even more complex with the introduction of little islands of rock without any soil on them. Among the finest examples of these are the ones in the Saihoji temple garden as

Joruriji temple garden

well as the crane islands in front of the Tenryuji temple garden waterfall. A small pond garden may dispense with a full-fledged island and make do with such rocky islets or a horseshoe-shaped promontory (one example being the Honen'in temple garden on p. 78). Since a promontory requires less shoreline than a full island, it has the advantage of making the pond look larger. Of course, there are also cases where even relatively large ponds may combine promontories and full islands to good effect. The "Pure Land" or *jodo-shiki* garden (Joruriji temple garden, for instance) is typical in this regard, with promontories on either side of the pond facing each other across an intervening island to represent the shores of this world versus the other.

Setting aside enough space for a sufficiently large island from the limited area available in a pond seems to have been a perennial challenge for garden designers past and present. The *Sakuteiki* states that though a large island is preferable, since it needs to be able to hold a musicians' pavilion at least twenty to twenty-five meters long, this may not always be possible; in such cases building a wooden platform as a temporary extension is recommended.

BRIDGES

The role of bridges in a pond garden can be significant. The effect they have depends greatly on such details as whether they are made of wood, stone, or earth, whether they have a railing or a roof, and whether they are flat or arched. Even among stone bridges there are various types: those made of cut or uncut stone and those using a single slab or several.

While the overall appearance of a bridge is important, individual components such as the foot of the bridge and the abutments joining the bridge to the shore are also features of note. The abutments receive more attention when a bridge is seen from a pleasure boat, while in the stroll garden the greater emphasis may be on the foot of the bridge.

YARIMIZU, NAGARE, AND WATERFALLS

These are some of the methods used to bring water into a pond garden.

Yarimizu are narrow, shallow streams that wind through the garden, as seen in scrolls depicting grand mansions of the Heian period. The stream was often made to flow southward from the east side of the main building in order to wash unfavorable spirits away toward the west as it went.

The *nagare*, a feature favored by the garden designer Ogawa Jihei, is another meandering stream, but wider in size, affording a better view of the flow of water within it.

The ideal means of irrigating a pond garden, however, is certainly the waterfall. The sight of water spilling down from above in configurations changing from one moment to the next is always attractive. A waterfall gives the surrounding air a sense of coolness, and even the rushing sound can be comforting to the ear. Sources such as the *Sakuteiki* reveal that the ancients strove hard to create a variety of waterfall effects, such as having two falls face each other (*mukai-ochi*); channeling the cascade along one side of a rock only (*kata-ochi*); or fanning the water out over a flat rock (*tsutai-ochi*).

THE DRY LANDSCAPE GARDEN

The *karesansui* garden consists primarily of stones. It is enclosed and introspective, in contrast to the brightness of a pond garden. Most dry landscape gardens are meant to be viewed from a sitting position inside a nearby building.

The Jukoin temple garden (pp. 26–27) and the garden of the Daishoin at Nishi Honganji temple (p. 36) are prototypical examples of this genre. The related term "rock garden" (examples of which are the Tokaian temple *tsuboniwa*, p. 81, the Hojo east garden of Ryogin'an temple, p. 49, and the Hojo south garden of Ryoanji temple) refers to a garden that contains neither water nor plantings but only stones arranged somewhat as in a *bonseki* tray arrangement. A *karesansui* stone arrangement (the upper garden at Saihoji temple, p. 86, for example) is a dry landscape that does not stand on its own as the center of interest but has been included in some other type of garden such as a pond garden. Though rocks are not a prominent part of either "sand gardens" (the Seiryo-den east courtyard at Kyoto Imperial Palace, p. 2) or "planting gardens" (the south garden of the main hall at Hokyoji temple, p. 65), the fact that they do not contain any water makes them special variants of the dry landscape garden.

Nishi Honganji temple (from *Miyako rinsen meisho zue*)

ORIGINS OF THE WORD *KARESANSUI*

The term is generally explained as originating in the idea of a landscape that has "dried up." The *Sakuteiki*, however, states that "when stones are set in a place with neither pond nor stream, this is called *karesansui*," suggesting that water was never actually part of the original plan.

In its earliest phase, the Japanese garden consisted of a pond with islands and stones arranged in water symbolizing the sea. This naturally meant that the base of all garden stones was submerged. The *karesansui* garden did away with this precept, placing the stones without any watercourse, so the bottom parts of the stones that would have been hidden by water were now visible—a condition that brought the word *karagu* to mind, referring to the way the ankles are revealed when the skirts of a kimono are raised. It is fair to assume that it is this word from which the term *karesansui* originated, particularly in view of the fact that the pronunciation was once *karasenzui*, which sounds even closer to *karagu*. Since this *kara* was written using several variant kanji, it can be inferred that its original meaning was not "dry" but some other sense common to these characters. "To reveal" is the only meaning that does not contradict any of the variants.

In short, *karesansui* can properly be defined as "a landscape of arranged stones whose bases, which would otherwise have been hidden by water, are revealed." It was from these beginnings, in conjunction with the influence of Zen Buddhism, that this style of garden developed.

The following are the standard compositional elements of a dry landscape garden.

CRANE AND TORTOISE

The gardens of the Nishi Honganji temple Daishoin (p. 36), Nanzenji Konchiin temple, and Tofukuji Fundain temple offer well-known examples of dry landscape gardens employing the crane and tortoise motif. No set rule seems to govern the position of the figures relative to each other, since in the first two gardens the crane is to the right and the tortoise to the left when viewed from the Shoin, while in the Fundain garden the placement is reversed. Although the choice may also have depended on topographical factors, the more prominent arrangement was often emphasized by placing it on the right-hand side, as most people in Japan tend to look toward the right first.

As to how to recognize the tortoise and the crane, the tortoise arrangement consists mainly of low stones in a horizontal configuration, while the crane arrangement makes use of standing stones with upward momentum suggesting wings and flight. The crane tends to be abstract and can be quite difficult to identify in a garden. The wings are not necessarily represented by two separate stones, and recognition is made even harder by the fact that the stones may symbolize more than one thing. For example, a stone that is flat and wide when placed upright may be used to symbolize the legendary Mt. Horai at the same time that it represents the wing of a crane. On the other hand,

Fundain temple garden

the tortoise is easier to locate because its stones are grouped in a circle and the head, tail, and feet are often depicted realistically. The head stone, which is often a distinctive reverse triangle in form, stands out especially well. Often placed at an angle, like that of a tortoise poking its head out of the water, the head stone makes this configuration relatively simple to pick out even from among a large number of stones.

The tortoise arrangement may also be recognized by the presence of one or two standing stones, called center stones, placed where the middle of the carapace would be. The inclination of these center stones signals the direction in which the tortoise is supposedly swimming: for example, if the center stones are slanted to the right, then the tortoise is headed toward the left. The crane arrangement can more easily be found by first identifying the tortoise by its head stone. The figure of a crane should then become evident somewhere nearby.

WATERFALLS

The waterfall is as important to the design of a dry landscape garden as it is to a pond garden. In the latter case, the cascade itself is the focal point, the role of the stones being to guide the water's descent. In the case of the dry landscape garden, no actual water flows, so stones are placed as devices to simulate the rush of water. Dynamic standing stones, therefore, are often used as cascade-supporting stones (*takizoe-ishi* or *fudo-ishi*) flanking the cascade stone (*mizuochi-ishi*) at the top of the falls. Between the supporting stones, a series of rocks with flat tops is arranged in descending steps, suggesting the downward movement of the cascade. The combination of the vertical lines of the standing stones and the sharp horizontal lines of the descending stones strengthens its impact.

STONE BRIDGES

In a dry landscape garden, a stone bridge is often set off by four bridge-supporting stones (*hashizoe-ishi*; also called "bridge-bracing" stones, *hashibasami-ishi*) at each of its four corners (though they may be omitted at one or two corners). Since the bridge may be visible from the side when seen from inside an adjacent building, without the presence of these stones the viewer might only be able to make out a horizontal bar-like shape. These stones not only make the bridge more recognizable but help to conceal the awkward transition between the ends of the bridge and the adjoining ground.

The allure of a bridge is in its role of linking places otherwise inaccessible. Symbolically, a bridge thus marks a barrier between this world and the ideal world on the other side. A dry landscape garden is at its most sublime when it allows the viewer to actually feel such boundaries can be crossed.

TRIAD STONES

Triad (*sanzon*) stones are set in a triangular arrangement suggesting the Buddhist trinity of a central Buddha figure and two supporting saints. The arrangement is formed by a relatively large stone (*chuson-seki*) in the center and two smaller attendant stones placed to the front on either side. Designs in which the two attendants line up on one side at the front and back of the center stone are referred to as horizontal triads. In dry landscape gardens, triads may also appear as part of the stones representing a waterfall or retaining an embankment. In some crane arrangements, triad stones simultaneously symbolize the wings and Mt. Horai.

The *Sakuteiki* mentions a "straddle" (*kohan*) stone arrangement similar to the triad arrangement. This is a stable and powerful pattern in which the center stone appears to straddle the two side stones. Arrangements of this type, seen in the gardens at Saihoji temple or Rokuonji Kinkaku pavilion, fell out of favor in later Japanese gardens, signaling the end of the *Sakuteiki*-style tradition and the decline of the art of stone arrangements.

BOAT STONES

A boat stone is an angular stone literally resembling a boat. Ideally it should have a pointed "bow" and a blunt "stern." According to Japanese tradition, boats symbolize more than a mere means of transportation, having connotations of both sanctity and fortune. A boat (known as the Ama no Iwafune) is the vessel of the gods in ancient mythology, and the seven deities of good fortune are said to bring wealth loaded on a boat. The bow of the boat stone should slant upward, like a tortoise-head stone, introducing an element of movement in an otherwise still landscape.

WHITE GRAVEL

White gravel or pebbles are an essential element for highlighting the stone arrangements in a dry landscape garden. The white gravel against gray rock makes a striking contrast and the use of somewhat finer, even-sized pebbles along the base of the stones brings their shape out more sharply. The very addition of white gravel moves a garden closer to perfection; indeed, without this element the dry landscape might never have reached the level of sophistication it has attained.

Made of weathered granite, the white pebbles produced in the Kitashirakawa area of Kyoto are nicely rounded and settle well when raked into patterns. Spread in a garden, they not only serve to express purity, the sunlight reflected off them forming a source of indirect light, but also to prevent the topsoil from blowing off as dust and to keep weeds from growing. Finally, patterns raked into the gravel give the garden a formality that discourages those not meant to enter from setting foot there.

INTERPLAY OF STONES AND EMPTY SPACE

Stone has been a source of awe and reverence for human beings since the dawn of history. People of ancient times felt a spiritual presence far beyond their comprehension in rocks that were regarded as the abodes of the gods. This reverence has been passed down through the ages, and explains why the dry landscape garden possesses an intrinsic power to stir the onlooker. It also explains why gardens such as that at Ryoanji temple, which might easily have been destroyed at some point, have instead been preserved over many centuries.

Understanding the silent, unassuming dry landscape garden is by no means easy. An attempt to grasp the symbolism of the stones by intellect alone may not be enough, and yet without acquiring some pertinent knowledge, one might gaze at them for hours to little effect. The best way to appreciate such a garden is ultimately to set aside one's acquired knowledge and commune silently with the scene, allowing one's inner spirit to respond to the aura emanating from the interplay of stones and empty space. Sitting in the posture of meditation also helps one to appreciate it.

THE TEA GARDEN

Although a garden without a teahouse is not, strictly speaking, a tea garden, many *tsuboniwa* adopt compositional techniques used in the tea garden, so that their appreciation follows many of the same principles.

THE GENESIS

The tea garden, like the *tsuboniwa*, has its origins in the spiritual dimension created within an enclosed space.

A passage in the early eleventh-century *Diary of Lady Murasaki* describing the difficulties in childbirth suffered by Empress Shoshi explains how women serving as mediums were individually surrounded by screens closed off with a curtain over the entrance, with a priest sitting in front of each, loudly chanting prayers to exorcise the spirits that possessed them. This account illustrates how a bounded space was considered necessary in dealing with the torments a person weakened by the labor of childbirth was undergoing.

The concept of enclosure also contains a sense of something furled, like an umbrella or a flower. The intrinsic qualities of what is furled do not change but only become smaller, more compact. The Japanese word for "enclose" is *tsubomu*, which is not only related to the word *tsuboniwa* but to *tsubonouchi*, the name given to earlier forms of the tea garden. Thus both types of garden originally embodied an effort to create a space filled with an unaccountable power through the act of enclosure.

Let us look at the structure and components employed to draw a line between the ordinary, mundane world and a realm on a higher plane.

INVITATION TO ANOTHER WORLD

One difference between the tea garden and the *tsuboniwa* lies in the former's preoccupation with time. A tea garden is intended to lead the visitor on a journey away from the mundane world, which is subject to the inexorable advance of time, into another realm that transcends it. The aim is to set aside the burdens of human toil and free the spirit from worldly attachments, or, put another way, to attain the spirit of a recluse abandoning the world of pain and suffering to live in quiet retirement in nature. Conceived not as a plane surface but as a continuous winding path that extends indefinitely onward, the tea garden seeks to reshape the visitor's sense of time. The pattern of continuity and repetition evident in stepping stones, so crucial to tea garden design, plays another trick with time. Stepping stones are not just meant to keep the visitors' feet clean, but to slow their advance as they move deeper into the world of the garden.

Spatially as well, a tea garden is devised so that its entirety cannot be taken in at one glance. The scene changes unexpectedly at selected points along the path, unsettling one's perspective and draw-

COMPONENTS OF A TEA GARDEN

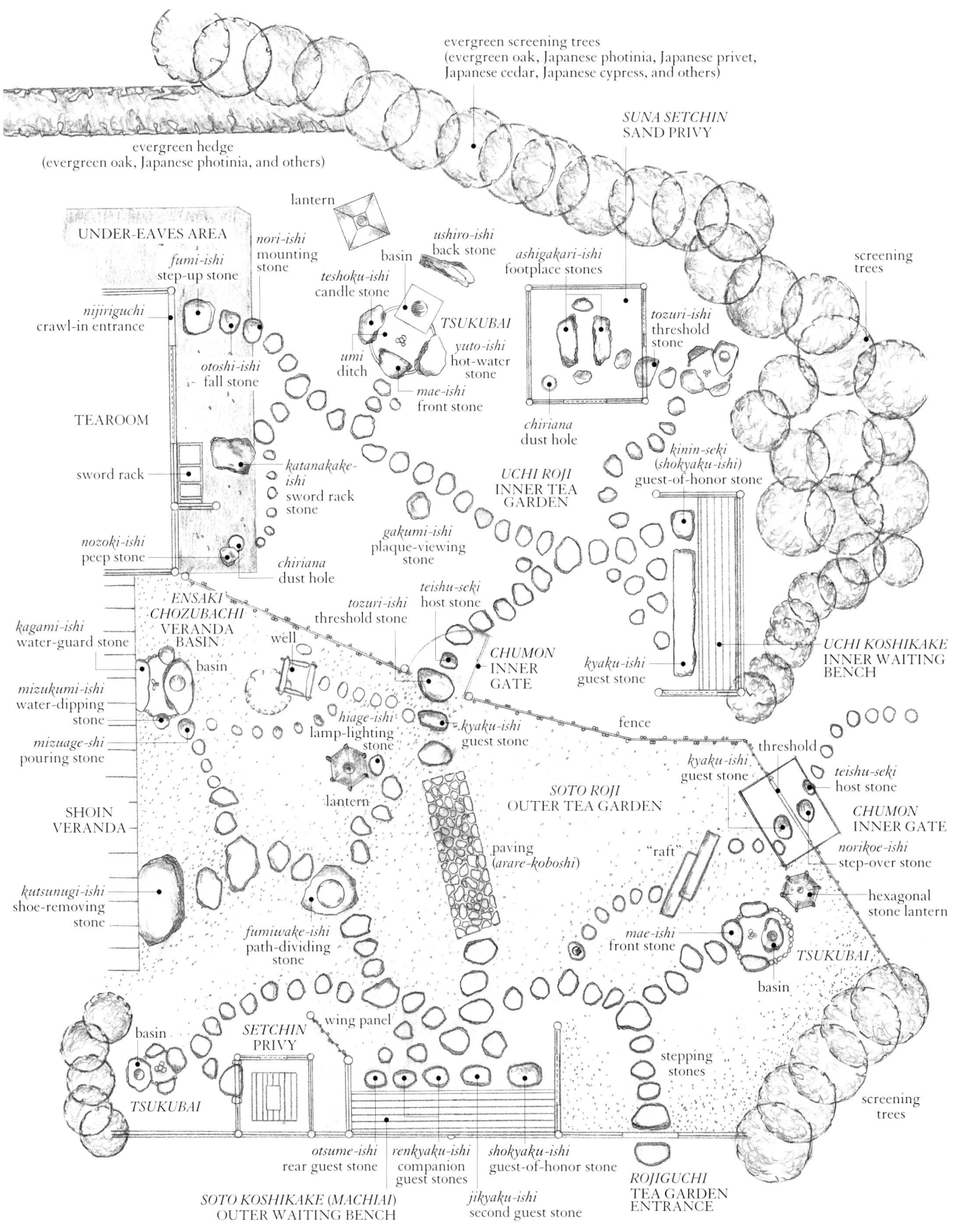

evergreen screening trees
(evergreen oak, Japanese photinia, Japanese privet,
Japanese cedar, Japanese cypress, and others)

SUNA SETCHIN
SAND PRIVY

evergreen hedge
(evergreen oak, Japanese photinia, and others)

screening
trees

lantern

UNDER-EAVES AREA

nori-ishi
mounting
stone

basin

ushiro-ishi
back stone

ashigakari-ishi
footplace stones

fumi-ishi
step-up stone

teshoku-ishi
candle stone

tozuri-ishi
threshold
stone

nijiriguchi
crawl-in entrance

TSUKUBAI

umi
ditch

yuto-ishi
hot-water
stone

otoshi-ishi
fall stone

mae-ishi
front stone

TEAROOM

chiriana
dust hole

kinin-seki
(*shokyaku-ishi*)
guest-of-honor stone

sword rack

katanakake-ishi
sword rack
stone

UCHI ROJI
INNER TEA
GARDEN

gakumi-ishi
plaque-viewing
stone

nozoki-ishi
peep stone

chiriana
dust hole

teishu-seki
host stone

ENSAKI
CHOZUBACHI
VERANDA
BASIN

tozuri-ishi
threshold stone

UCHI KOSHIKAKE
INNER WAITING
BENCH

kagami-ishi
water-guard stone

well

kyaku-ishi
guest stone

CHUMON
INNER
GATE

basin

mizukumi-ishi
water-dipping
stone

hiage-ishi
lamp-lighting
stone

kyaku-ishi
guest stone

fence

threshold

kyaku-ishi
guest stone

mizuage-shi
pouring stone

lantern

SOTO ROJI
OUTER TEA GARDEN

teishu-seki
host stone

SHOIN
VERANDA

"raft"

CHUMON
INNER GATE

norikoe-ishi
step-over stone

kutsunugi-ishi
shoe-removing
stone

paving
(*arare-koboshi*)

hexagonal
stone lantern

fumiwake-ishi
path-dividing
stone

mae-ishi
front stone

TSUKUBAI

basin

basin

SETCHIN
PRIVY

wing panel

stepping
stones

screening
trees

TSUKUBAI

otsume-ishi
rear guest stone

renkyaku-ishi
companion
guest stones

shokyaku-ishi
guest-of-honor stone

ROJIGUCHI
TEA GARDEN
ENTRANCE

jikyaku-ishi
second guest stone

SOTO KOSHIKAKE (MACHIAI)
OUTER WAITING BENCH

ing one deeper into the unordinary. The broadleaf evergreens (evergreen oak and holly, for example) commonly found in tea gardens serve not only the purpose of physical concealment but provide a discreet cloak of greenery that prevents the visitor's attention from straying outside as well. Plantings intended for this function naturally avoid trees that flower.

Indeed, no flowers bloom in the tea garden, since they would only remind the visitor of the movement of the seasons. After having passed through this colorless, timeless realm, however, the flower the visitor then encounters—the one arranged in the alcove (*tokonoma*) of the tearoom—assumes a significance far beyond that of any ordinary blossom. It becomes a symbol of pure existence, a flower that does not fade or wither but blooms forever frozen in one eternal moment.

These features, along with other tea garden conventions such as the waiting area, inner gate, and water basin, work together to form a retreat from the world that has taken centuries to perfect.

WAITING AREA

The guests invited to a tea ceremony first gather in a waiting area. Technically called the "waiting space" (*machiai*) when located in the outer tea garden and "waiting bench" (*koshikake*) when in the inner garden, this may be referred to generally as a *koshikake machiai* or simply *machiai*. The step below the waiting seat reserved for the guest of honor is called the *shokyaku-ishi* and those for other guests are *kyaku-ishi*. There are various seating arrangements, but in cases where the guests are lined up in a row, the guest-of-honor stone is typically larger, higher, and in a more forward position than the stones for the other seats. The guest-of-honor stone is positioned to line up with the center of the principal guest's seat, which may take up about a quarter of the length of the bench, with the rest of the space divided equally between the remaining visitors. For these other guests, a long stone or paving may sometimes take the place of individual guest stones.

INNER GATE

The *chumon*, which marks the entrance to the inner tea garden, may be an elaborate structure with a substantial roof or just a simple wicket. The host stands on the host stone (*teishu-seki*) inside the gate while greeting guests proceeding from the waiting area to the guest stone (*kyaku-ishi*) located outside the gate opposite the host stone. If the gate has a sill, then a step-over stone (*norikoe-ishi*) lying in front of the host stone helps the guests over the threshold. If there is no sill, then there is a threshold stone (*tozuri-ishi*) placed in the middle of the gate in between the host and guest stones. The host stone is typically smaller and lower than either the step-over or the guest stones.

WATER BASINS

The *tsukubai* is an indispensable component of a tea garden, consisting of a "stooping basin," so called because guests must stoop to rinse their hands and mouth here before entering the tearoom, and a front stone or *mae-ishi* for them to stand on, with stepping stones leading the way to it. The basin and front stone are a mandatory pair, unlike more optional elements such as the candle stone (*teshoku-ishi*) or hot-water stone (*yuto-ishi*). The former is for holding candles used when tea ceremonies are performed in the evening, while a bucket of warm water may be placed by the basin on the hot-water stone for use in winter. Given their functions, both types of stone are naturally flat. The Omote Senke style prefers to position the candle stone on the left side of the basin, while the Ura Senke style more frequently places the hot-water stone on that side. Both also serve to prevent erosion of the ditch (called the *umi*, literally "sea") dug between the basin and the front stone in order to drain off any spilled water.

These various functional stones are artfully combined with the basin to create an aesthetic impact that surpasses the sum of the parts. The relatively small size of the individual objects makes them especially appropriate for tea gardens and *tsuboniwa*, whose limited space prevents the introduction of very large rocks. It is hardly surprising that these compact elements, along with stone lanterns, which are also relatively easy to transport, are the components most often used in tea garden and *tsuboniwa* design.

CRAWL-IN ENTRANCE

The *nijiriguchi* is the entrance to the tearoom from the tea garden. The guest steps up to the entrance on a flat stone called the step-up stone (*fumi-ishi*) or sometimes the "first stone" (*ichiban-ishi*), placed immediately in front of the entrance. Though the placement of this stone varies according to its height and distance vis-à-vis the entrance, the rule of thumb is that it be gauged so that the guest's knees come up to the level of the threshold when stooping to move inside. Once the height of the stone has been determined in relation to the threshold, other stones are used to ease the step up to this stone from the path. The stone placed down one step from the first stone is called the second or "fall" stone (*otoshi-ishi*), followed by the third or "mounting" stone (*nori-ishi*), and from then on to the stepping stones, the difference in height diminishing progressively.

Other components of tea garden design include the privy (*setchin*), stone lantern, bamboo fence, hedge, well, sword rack and accompanying stone, dust hole (*chiriana*, into which sweepings are emptied), paving, stepping stones, and path-dividing stone (*fumiwake-ishi*).

Various fences

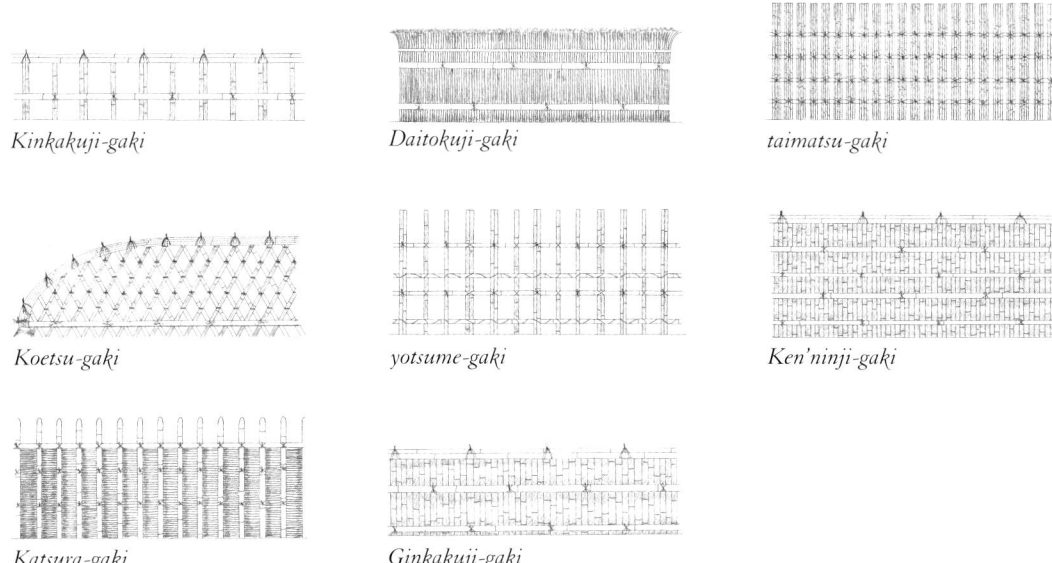

Kinkakuji-gaki *Daitokuji-gaki* *taimatsu-gaki*

Koetsu-gaki *yotsume-gaki* *Ken'ninji-gaki*

Katsura-gaki *Ginkakuji-gaki*

MOSS

Moss is as indispensable to the tea garden as is white gravel to the dry landscape. It may be no exaggeration to say that the host devotes the most time and attention to caring for the moss, which is surprisingly difficult to maintain. Though moss needs moisture in order to flourish, if it becomes too damp the ugly liverwort (Marchantia polymorpha), a type of lichen, may sprout up instead. Only diligent care, such as thinning the cover of the trees overhead, regular watering, and above all meticulous cleaning using small hand brooms, will achieve the appropriate humidity, sunlight, and air required for attractive growth.

In the case of haircap moss, one of the leading types of moss used in a Japanese garden, the above conditions coincide with a need to restrain its growth so that it continues to appear short and full. Trimming haircap moss is best done in the spring during the cherry blossom season, after the frosts have passed. At this time the buds recover quickly and there is no fear that low temperature, always the worst enemy of moss, will cause the ground to freeze over.

Care must be taken not to damage the moss when visiting a tea garden, since it represents the result of many long years of work. Soft-soled shoes are preferred, and those with high heels should be avoided at all costs.

Quiet and deeply soothing, moss can look like a miraculous carpet laid over the surface of the garden. It is doubtful whether Kyoto's tea gardens would have been so luminously beautiful or its *tsuboniwa* so well loved without the presence of moss. Many now famous gardens, deprived of much of their charm, might have simply been allowed to fade away if moss had not unfolded its charms in them.

■　■　■

There are many ways to enjoy a garden. Its stones, its trees and shrubs, and even the ferns and moss offer silent testimony to the deep resources of nature. Autumn leaves may flutter down one by one to gently rest upon the ground, or a breeze may shake down a flurry that covers the earth with color. What feelings such sights arouse differ from person to person. Regardless of what we might see there, a garden affords a means for the expression of something that otherwise has no tangible form.

（英文版）京都秘蔵の庭
The Hidden Gardens of Kyoto

2004 年 7 月　第 1 刷発行
2004 年12月　第 2 刷発行

写　真　水野克比古
文　　　小埜雅章
発行者　畑野文夫
発行所　講談社インターナショナル株式会社
　　　　〒112-8652 東京都文京区音羽 1-17-14
　　　　電話　03-3944-6493（編集部）
　　　　　　　03-3944-6492（営業部・業務部）
　　　　ホームページ　www.kodansha-intl.com

印刷・製本所　株式会社サンエムカラー

落丁本・乱丁本は購入書店名を明記のうえ、小社業務部宛にお送
りください。送料小社負担にてお取替えします。なお、この本に
ついてのお問い合わせは、編集部宛にお願いいたします。本書の
無断複写（コピー）、転載は著作権法の例外を除き、禁じられてい
ます。

定価はカバーに表示してあります。

Copyright © 2004 by Katsuhiko Mizuno and Masaaki Ono
Printed in Japan
ISBN 4-7700-2937-3